PRAISE FOR *ONE MINUTE STEWARDSHIP SERMONS*

"Charles Cloughen has fashioned a heartwarming argument in favor of giving money as the way of having money—not so much as a way of having more... but of enjoying it more for learning to practice a relationship to money that transforms anxiety into gratitude.... [This book's] careful study will enhance any Christian's ministry and boost the vitality of any congregation."
—*Bennett J. Sims*
  Bishop Emeritus of Atlanta and author of Servanthood:
  Leadership for the Third Millennium

"An excellent practical, hands-on tool for year-round stewardship of money for Baby Boomers, based on a theology of thanksgiving and gratitude."
—*Bill Easum*
  Author of Church Growth Handbook *and coauthor of*
  Growing Spiritual Redwoods

"Cloughen combines biblically based theology with practical communication methods. The book is at once a compass for stewardship preaching and a resource for one-minute, year-round stewardship meditations."
—*Herb Miller*
  Editor of Net Results: New Ideas in Church Vitality

MORE PRAISE...

"I find [*One Minute Stewardship Sermons*] to be perhaps the only guidebook available on assisting clergy to integrate 'every-Sunday stewardship teachings' into the worship life of the congregation. We needed this kind of wisdom a hundred years ago."
—*Tom Gossen*
Executive Director
The Episcopal Network for Stewardship

"I especially like how many of the one-minute sermons affirm and thank members of the congregation for their gifts. Acknowledging how we are blessed is a first step to living the life of a steward."
—*Susan Graham Walker*
Stewardship Education Consultant of the Anglican Diocese of Toronto and coauthor of God, Kids, and Us

"The messages give a fresh approach...to giving and incorporate it into the worship as a meaningful part of the service. The messages also inspire the contributor to present tithes and offerings with a better understanding of God's work on planet Earth. They are good when used in the church bulletin."
—*Avery N. Penn*
Pastor, Mount Olive Baptist Church
United Baptist Missionary Convention
National Baptist Convention, U.S.A., Inc.

MORE PRAISE...

"Charles Cloughen, from his wealth of experience as a parish priest and stewardship leader, has offered in this book a great gift to the Church!"
—*The Reverend Roy W. Cole*
  Episcopal Pastor

"This fine book is packed with short, poignant, and pertinent reminders about the true 'whys' of giving... as a spiritual act done in thanksgiving in order to enable the mission/ministry versus paying the maintenance bills."
—*Marlene Wilson*
  President of the Volunteer Management Association and
  author of How to Mobilize Church Volunteers

"Clear...to the point...gives practical examples and suggestions...provides material that can be used immediately—as is!"
—*The Right Reverend C. L. Longest*
  Suffragan Bishop of the Episcopal Diocese of Maryland

"Here's a fresh approach on how to say thank you to your congregation fifty-two Sundays a year for their time, talents, and money. A book you can keep on your shelf and scan through for ideas year after year."
—*Catherine Ritter*
  Director of Family Life
  Towson United Methodist Church
  Towson, Maryland

MORE PRAISE...

"We have watched Father Cloughen preach and teach on stewardship for more than a decade. This work captures his spiritual yet organized method of communicating the essence of Christian stewardship. *One Minute* is practical and inspiring."
−*Glenn and Barbara Holliman*
  Authors of With Generous Hearts
  and The Complete Planned Giving Kit

"Father Cloughen's creativity, commitment, and experience persuasively and convincingly lead me, as reader and rector, to many useful ideas, projects, and short sermon topics. I know that I will use his book regularly to plan programming and preaching. I recommend this book to clergy and lay leaders for their reading and use."
−*Ron Reed*
  Rector, St. James Episcopal Church, Wichita, Kansas
  Past National Stewardship Officer of the Episcopal Church

"Talking about stewardship throughout the year can seem an overwhelming challenge. Father Cloughen makes that not only achievable, but informational and inspiring, as well. His examples should help others create their own sound bites that will help their congregations understand this aspect of Christian life."
−*Terry Parsons*
  National Stewardship· Officer, The Episcopal Church

"This book is a tremendous resource for bulletins, sermons, and thoughts that really make a difference. I've used it over and over and the well never runs dry."
−*The Reverend Michael Curry*
  Rector, St. James Church, Baltimore, Maryland

MORE PRAISE...

"Since stewardship, as Cloughen reminds us, is the way we manage our lives, including our money, the subject calls for continuing emphasis. Year-round stewardship education is essential if our people are to grow in awareness and response. This little book can help communicate the stewardship message every Sunday of the year."
–Harris W. Lee
  Stewardship Consultant
  (from Augsburg Fortress Book Newsletter, Winter 1997)

"I would heartily recommend this book to Christian pastors. In reading it, I was continually reminded of opportunities that might be used to educate people in giving and also to express appreciation for faithful use of gifts."
–The Reverend Frederick K. Weimert
  Calvary Baptist Church, Towson, Maryland
  Former President, American Baptist Churches of the South

"Christian stewardship is a daily way of life that requires education and community support. Father Cloughen's book, which features weekly examples for parish education and worship, is a wonderful liturgical aid for those who want to assist their congregation in this important work."
–The Reverend Phebe L. McPhearson
  Rector, Epiphany Episcopal Church, Odenton, Maryland

ONE
MINUTE
STEWARDSHIP
SERMONS

Charles Cloughen Jr.

MOREHOUSE PUBLISHING

Morehouse Publishing
P.O. Box 1321
Harrisburg, PA 17105

Morehouse Publishing is a Continuum imprint.

Library of Congress Cataloging-in-Publication Data

Cloughen, Charles.
    One minute stewardship sermons / Charles Cloughen, Jr.
      p. cm.
    Includes bibliographical references.
    ISBN 0-8192-1720-4 (paper)
    1. Stewardship, Christian–Sermons. 2. Christian giving–Sermons.
  3. Sermons, American. I. Title.
    BV772.C57 1997
    248'.6–dc21
                                      97-27224
                                          CIP

Printed in the United States of America

First Edition
3 5 7 9 10 8 6

CONTENTS

ACKNOWLEDGMENTS

I once heard of a person who, when he was honored for his accomplishments, responded: "I stood on the shoulders of giants!" That is the way I feel regarding this book, *One Minute Stewardship Sermons.* I am standing on the shoulders of so many others and benefiting from their vision, passion, and teaching.

My good friend and colleague Robert Daly has a wonderful quotation that he has taught me: "All great ideas normally degenerate into hard work."

This book would not have been published without the hard work and help of:

My wife, Judy, whose unfailing patience, whose understanding of the many hours of reading and writing necessary to bring this book to completion, whose encouragement during the long days of waiting to hear from the publishers, and whose constant support and love were invaluable in every phase of midwifing the final product.

Our secretary at Saint Thomas's, Karen Ermer, who took my longhand notes, typed and edited them, and then re-typed them into my first draft.

Elizabeth Huntress, my mother-in-law, who was my patient and hardworking primary editor and who prepared the final draft.

Deborah Grahame, my editor at Morehouse Publishing, who worked with me over the course of two years and who is responsible for the publication of the book.

The Virginia Theological Seminary, Alexandria, Virginia, where I spent my sabbatical in an apartment, reading and reflecting, as I wrote the first draft of this book.

Heartfelt thanks also should go:

To my father, Charles, who always pledged to the church and who taught me the habit of being a faithful giver.

To my mother, Anna, who sacrificed so that I could attend Hobart College and who encouraged my journey into the priesthood and the Episcopal Church.

To an inspiration from Charles Wilson, Church Planner, whose off-hand comment gave me the idea to produce the wonderful bumper sticker: "If you love Jesus, Tithe! Anyone can honk!"

To Oscar Carr, past Episcopal National Stewardship Officer, who invited me to the Jacksonville, Florida, Province IV's Stewardship Conference, funded by the Episcopal Church Foundation and Trinity Church, Wall Street, New York, NY. These conferences began a "Renaissance of Stewardship" in the Episcopal Church.

To the Rev. Canon David Crockett, retired, who taught me the "three-sided coin"—one side, stewardship; one side, evangelism; and bounded by education—explaining that these three can never be separated.

To Thomas Carson, retired National Officer for the Episcopal Church, who assembled a wonderful team to teach stewardship, and happily, included me as a member of his team.

To James Annand, retired, Dean of Berkeley Divinity School at Yale, who, along with Harold Whiteman, taught me about development and seminary support at a national level.

To Ronald Reed, Past PECUSA National Stewardship Officer, now Rector of St. James Church, Wichita, Kansas, who taught, encouraged, and mentored me.

To George Regas, retired pastor of All Saints Church, Pasadena, California, who introduced me to the concept of using the time of the offertory sentence as a stewardship teaching moment.

To Frederick Jellison, retired rector of Saint James Church, Woonsocket, Rhode Island, who taught me my role as a pastor and priest acting as both stewardship leader and teacher.

To Frederick Osborn, the Director of Planned Giving for the Episcopal Church Foundation, who taught me about the ministry of planned giving.

To the Vestry and parishioners of:
- Saint Martin's Church, Providence, Rhode Island, and the Rev. Halsey Dewolfe Howe
- Saint Matthew's Church, Jamestown, Rhode Island
- Saint John's Church, Waterbury, Connecticut, and the Rev. James Wilson
- Saint Andrew's Church, Pasadena, Maryland

My special thanks goes to the members of Saint Thomas's Church, where I have been serving as rector since 1990. They generously gave me a sabbatical in which to write this book. And to my colleagues, Austin Schildwachter and Michael Mayor, who have encouraged me to pursue and supported me in my stewardship journey!

My special thanks to those who accepted my invitation to be readers for *One Minute Stewardship Sermons;* they made this book possible.

The Rev. Roy W. Cole
Pastor
Interim Specialist for Revitalization
Diocese of Maryland

Dr. Amelia Geary
Director of the Center for Teaching
Virginia Theological Seminary
Alexandria, Virginia

The Rt. Rev. Robert Ihloff
Bishop of the Episcopal Diocese of Maryland

The Rt. Rev. Charles C.L. Longest
Suffragan Bishop of the Episcopal Diocese of Maryland
Past Member of the General Convention's Standing Commission
   on Stewardship and Development

The Rev. Michael Mayor
Assistant, St. Thomas's Episcopal Church
Towson, Maryland

The Rev. Mary Morgan
Pastor of the Maryland Presbyterian Church, USA
Towson, Maryland

Frederick Osborn
Director of Planned Giving
Episcopal Church Foundation
New York, New York

The Rev. Ronald Reed
Pastor
Saint James Episcopal Church
Wichita, Kansas

Catherine Ritter
Director of Family Life
Towson United Methodist Church
Towson, Maryland

The Rev. Tim Wright
Executive Pastor of the Community Church of Joy
Evangelical Lutheran Church of America
Phoenix, Arizona

CONTRIBUTORS

The Rev. Phebe Coe
Pastor of the Church of the
  Epiphany
Odenton, Maryland

The Rev. Roy W. Cole
Pastor
Interim Specialist for Revitalization
Diocese of Maryland

Canon David W. Crockett
Episcopal Diocese of Western
  Massachusetts

Dr. Amelia Geary
Director for the Center for
  Teaching
Virginia Theological Seminary
Alexandria, Virginia

The Rt. Rev. Robert Ihloff
Bishop
Episcopal Diocese of Maryland

The Rt. Rev. Charles C.L. Longest
Suffragan Bishop
Episcopal Diocese of Maryland
Past Member of the General
  Convention's Standing
  Commission on Stewardship
  and Development

The Rt. Rev. George Mocko
Bishop of Delaware-Maryland
  Synod
Evangelical Lutheran Church
  in America

The Rev. Mary Morgan
Pastor of Maryland Presbyterian
  Church, U.S.A.
Towson, Maryland

Frederick Osborn
Director of Planned Giving
Episcopal Church Foundation
New York, New York

The Rev. Ronald Reed
Pastor of St. James Episcopal
  Church
Wichita, Kansas

Catherine Ritter
Director of Family Life
Towson United Methodist Church
Towson, Maryland

The Rev. Tim Wright
Executive Pastor of the
  Community Church of Joy
Evangelical Lutheran Church in
  America
Phoenix, Arizona

(A listing of each person's contributions appears in the index, page 118.)

FOREWORD

IN THE FALL OF THE YEAR, many pastors, some of them begrudgingly, turn their attention to the subject of stewardship. Many pastors I know dread this, but it seems inevitable. Many lay people dread this time as well–dread the time when they will be called upon to be stewardship visitors or simply called upon to be asked for their pledge. Others in the church dread this time of year because they will hear stewardship sermons that may make them feel uncomfortable. We live in a culture and attend churches where talking about money and talking about giving do not come easily and frequently do not come joyfully.

In recent years, a new trend has developed in many churches–the idea of talking about stewardship at any time of year, at all times of year. Year-round stewardship has become the goal of many congregations and some denominations. This trend is not designed simply to increase giving to the church, although this couldn't hurt; rather, it is an attempt to recognize that stewardship lies at the very heart of Christian living and a Christian understanding of our possessions. Stewardship is about investing; investing is an exciting thing for most people because we expect a return. Our stewardship investing brings returns as well, and they come out of our response to a loving God who has invested in us and in our world.

One Minute Stewardship Sermons is an excellent resource compiled and written by the Rev. Charles Cloughen. The book itself makes the point that stewardship is in season in all seasons; that there is no occasion and no Christian gathering in which a timely reminder of the importance of stewardship need be out of place. In fact, it is far more effective for pastors continuously to remind their congregations of the importance and centrality of stewardship. How we invest what we have has a great deal to do with our spiritual well-being. Jesus makes this point in many of his parables and in many other of his sayings. It is often forgotten in the church and, therefore, it is of even greater importance that we take seriously the effect that our material well-being has on our spiritual health. The people who feel spiritually whole are almost always those who have found exciting ways in which to invest their resources, ways that bespeak their faith and the priorities that they hold dear. Such people are cheerful givers.

A central job for pastors in the church is to help to create a larger number of cheerful givers. *One Minute Stewardship Sermons* is an excellent resource for ideas on how stewardship can be communicated in a very short period of time on a regular basis, Sunday to Sunday, Christian gathering to Christian gathering.

Finally, here is a practical resource to be used by pastors and preachers for communication of stewardship at any time and at all times of the year.

The Rt. Rev. Robert W. Ihloff
Episcopal Bishop of Maryland

PREFACE

STEWARDSHIP IS THANKSGIVING. Giving thanks for all God has given us: all of our time, our abilities, and our money. Stewardship is how we manage our entire lives and includes what we give back to God for His work throughout the church. One minute stewardship sermons may be incorporated into the regular Sunday sermon or printed in the bulletin, but they are primarily designed to stand alone and be given at the time of the offertory.

With these stewardship sermons, through a hundred different illustrations, stewardship leaders in the Christian church connect the mission and vision of the local church with the stewardship of the church members' time, ability, and money. These sermons will be especially effective for the "Boomers," the "X-Generation," and the un-churched or newly-churched members.

The sermons are organized: first, in a general way, by Scripture; second, by the Church Year; and third, by topic. They are offered as illustrations of how one can make use of stewardship sermons in the context of the regular Sunday or weekday worship service. They are cross-indexed in the appendix.

INTRODUCTION

HAVE YOU EVER heard of Crest®? I believe that if one asked 100 people this question, 98 would reply, "Sure! You mean Crest® toothpaste." Why does Procter & Gamble® spend millions of dollars a year to tell us about Crest® by offering brief commercials frequently throughout the year? If they really want to get their message out, why don't they buy a half hour block of prime time television to tell the Crest® story?

This simple illustration from the secular world helps to teach us something about stewardship. Church members pledge and give for the ministry of the church and not to pay parish bills or to reduce a deficit, in the same way that they buy Crest® to protect their teeth, not to help pay bills for Procter & Gamble®.

Loading an entire yearly stewardship message into one annual 20-minute sermon is equivalent to Proctor & Gamble's® loading their entire yearly advertising message into one commercial in the fall.

There is a better way.

In many Christian churches, a most awkward moment comes before and during the Offertory Sentence. Many clergy and other leaders of worship ignore this moment to teach and miss the chance every week to continue stewardship education at an opportune point in the service. The Offertory Sentences and the time used in preparing the elements for communion are a natural lead-in to stewardship education. I often suggest this concept to other clergy, saying, "There is a way to make use of these awkward moments–the stewardship sermon. Try one; you might be pleasantly surprised." And they have found that the suggestion works.

My epiphany came some 20 years ago, during an Episcopal Stewardship Conference in Attleboro, Massachusetts, sponsored by the Episcopal Church's National Stewardship

Office. At this workshop, one speaker, the Rev. George Regas, pastor of All Saints Episcopal Church, Pasadena, California, mentioned what he did at the Offertory. He explained to us that he talked about money–stating that the clergy are accused of doing that anyway–and used this time to explain the ministry that was being done by the church with the money that the members pledged and gave each week.

Over these past 20 years, I have worked to expand his idea and to develop the concept of connecting money and ministry in the areas of stewardship and planned giving. During the majority of the services, I give one of my one minute stewardship sermons, connecting what each person and family gives– in the way of time, abilities, and money–with the ministry of the church. I do this in the spirit of thanksgiving, rather than begging. It transforms the Offertory Sentences into a time of joy and thanksgiving for God's gifts given to us. I connect these stewardship sermons to our mission and vision, which, at St. Thomas's Church, is to worship and serve in Jesus' name.

This time of teaching, week by week, is crucial if we are to educate the hearts and minds of the "Boomers," the "Generation Xers," and the newly churched members on the principles and practices of giving. The future of our churches depends on the conversion of the these generations to a generation of those who give generously of their time, abilities, and money to God's work that is being accomplished through the greater church. Their future depends on their realizing the need to give generously of themselves, sharing what they have with others in the building of a Christian community.

One of the greatest challenges for the church (local, regional, and national) is communicating its mission and vision.

In my congregation, I know that if I place a notice of an event in the monthly newsletter, in the Sunday bulletin, and on our two bulletin boards, about 50 percent of the church members will remember and know it is happening. In the 21st century, a church that relies merely on the written word will be in trouble.

One Minute Stewardship Sermons is designed to help meet the challenge our churches face for the 21st century in communicating stewardship to those under fifty, many of whom have no history of *duty* to the church. Experience has taught me that people enter the church (the unchurched; these are people who have never been members of a church and who are totally unfamiliar with church tradition) or reenter the church (the dischurched; these are persons who, at some time in their lives, attended church and who, after an absence, are now returning to attend regularly) at low giving levels.

Then, if good stewardship teaching takes place, they increase their giving to support the mission and vision of the local and greater church. I believe this increase comes out of their God-given need to give. They will not support the local church merely out of duty, and so the local church cannot survive. Also, appealing merely to people to give to reduce the deficit or to meet the budget offers little or no attraction, either for these new givers or for our regular congregation. In itself, the need of the church to survive has little appeal for anyone.

Our local churches have to develop a solid mission and vision and communicate this vision week by week so that the worshippers will be eager to give of their time, talent, and money to make that vision happen. Our denominations, if they are going to survive and prosper, need to build and then communicate a mission and vision that will move local vestries, councils, and governing boards to give their time, ability, and money to support the larger vision and mission. Local congregations will respond with their stewardship appeals for local mission initiatives such as food pantries, soup kitchens, and shelters for abused women and pregnant teenagers. In most cases, these projects are ecumenically based.

In my denomination, we sometimes practice a pairing of congregations. In our diocese, the strategy for the 21st century is the pairing of affluent suburban congregations with inner city congregations, sharing resources to "make disciples of all nations." This is not following the old model of sending money to missions, but a true partnership—exchanging choirs and clergy—creating a true two-way street. Concepts such as these will give the church goer of the 21st century superior hands-on ministry opportunities.

The teaching of stewardship is actually the making of faithful disciples of Jesus Christ. These stewardship sermons are designed to be used to thank people for their part in making good things happen—not only talking about the future, but also acknowledging their support of time, talent, and money, Sunday after Sunday, in making possible the many ministries that our local, regional, and national churches are providing.

One Minute Stewardship Sermons was created by taking a personal theology of stewardship and connecting it to the mission and vision of the ministry of the congregation or institution we serve, when we *thank* the people for what they have *already* accomplished by giving of their time, abilities, and money.

This book deals first with building a theological foundation based on biblical theology and stewardship—a foundation based on abundance not scarcity, a foundation based on an appreciation of God's abundant gifts that we have already received. Second, it deals with guidelines on how best to construct these sermons. And the third major section offers examples written by outstanding stewardship leaders from many denominations, which may be used as written or serve as inspiration in writing your own stewardship sermons.

TERMINOLOGY

THIS BOOK IS WRITTEN from my own experiences as a pastor in the Episcopal Church. However, I hope it will be helpful for all who want to work for stronger stewardship, whatever your denomination. To help make the concepts in this book more easily understood by everyone, some of the terms that are used in the following pages are defined.

First, the head clergy person of a congregational ministry in the Episcopal Church is called a *rector* or *vicar*. In the Episcopal Church, too, most clergy who fulfill a pastoral function are priests. In many Episcopal churches, male priests are called *Father*. Unfortunately, we do not have a commonly agreed upon term for a woman priest. "Mother" has not been widely accepted, so one finds a confusion between terms such as Father Smith and Mrs. Smith, Father Jim and Blanche. Thus, for the purposes of this book, the Lutheran term for a clergy member–*pastor*–is used. It is gender neutral and denotes well the function of our priesthood within the local church.

The *vestry* is the Episcopal term for a parish's legal governing board within the life of the congregation. In other denominations, this corresponds to such titles as Trustees, Deacons, Parish Council, Administrative Board, or Session. Church members of Episcopal churches are called *parishioners,* since in our nomenclature, the church is called a *parish*. In the past, the parish was defined as a geographic area of the church's local ministry, but now, many parishioners cross over to other parishes to worship in a church which they believe better meets their needs.

All local Episcopal churches belong to a *diocese,* a geographical area that normally is named after a state–The Diocese of Maryland–or after part of a state or city–The Diocese of Dallas. The head of the diocese is the *bishop* elected by a convention composed of the clergy and elected lay representatives from each congregation. The bishop corresponds to the area head of any denomination, and dioceses correspond to the greater structure of other types of association. The Episcopal Church is a confederation of 99 domestic and 14 overseas dioceses that meet regularly in a General Convention every three years.

I hope you will find this book helpful, whether you are a pastor, a worship leader, a stewardship chairman, a member of a stewardship committee, or a faithful member of a church concerned about your own and your church's stewardship.

(All scripture text, unless noted, is from the New Revised Standard Version, *Harper Collins Study Bible.*)

DEVELOPING YOUR PERSONAL THEOLOGY OF STEWARDSHIP

Section I

SECTION I
Developing Your Personal Theology of Stewardship

DO YOU REALLY BELIEVE that God will provide for you and your family's needs? In the Sermon on the Mount, Jesus tells us:

> "Give, and it will be given to you. A good measure, pressed down, shaken together, running over, will be put into your lap; for the measure you give will be the measure you get back." *–Luke 6:38*

God is generous, giving, loving, forgiving, and gracious. God desires our loving response to His generosity. In reading books on stewardship, what stands out for me is the personal witness of the writer, who has been the recipient of God's generosity. I have not always given generously to God through the church, but my wife Judy and I have been generously blessed. God's generosity can be seen most clearly in retrospect. Examine your life. Search to see God's generous hand in it. Take out a pad of paper and write down the times in your life or in the lives of others close to you when God's hand has been present. Keep these examples. They will make wonderful illustrations for your stewardship teaching and preaching.

Now think of some times when your congregation has stepped out in faith and God has been there. Jot down these times and save them; they too will be wonderful stewardship sermons.

> *When we have acted faithfully and responsively,*
> *God has provided.*

A quotation from the Rev. Sara Chandler, adjunct professor of stewardship at the Virginia Theological Seminary, states: "God doesn't order what God won't pay for!"

Stewardship is thanksgiving, giving thanks for all that God has given us–our time, our abilities, and our money. Stewardship is the way we manage *all* our time, abilities, and money. Nothing of value happens in human life without these three currencies. Nothing of value happens in the life of a church without these three currencies. Some think of stewardship as what we give, or return, to God for His work through the church; they teach that the tithe means 10 percent of our worldly goods. I believe that 100 percent is God's.

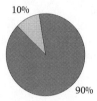

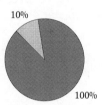

90% Ours
10% God's Work

100% God's
10% God's Work

Our stewardship is our decision as to how we live and manage our entire life. What we return to God through the church is only a part of our stewardship. We are given by God the freedom to manage all of our time, abilities, and money. That process of management is called stewardship.

Are You A Good Steward?

The first key to good stewardship in a congregation is the pastor.
1. Is the pastor comfortable about money?
2. Does the pastor tithe?
3. Is the pastor comfortable about preaching and teaching about money and the tithe?

Is Tithing Christian? Is It Biblical?

If one examines the Hebrew scriptures, one finds many explanations of tithes and offerings. In Genesis, Abram is blessed by Melchizedek after he brings his tithe to the priest.

> After his return from the defeat of Chedorlaomer and the kings who were with him, the king of Sodom went out to meet him at the Valley of Shaveh (that is, the King's Valley). And King Melchizedek of Salem brought out bread and wine; he was priest of God Most High. He blessed him and said, "Blessed be Abram by God Most High, maker of heaven and earth; And blessed be God Most High, who has delivered your enemies into your hand!" And Abram gave him one tenth of everything. —*Genesis 14:17-20*

In Deuteronomy, Chapter 14, the Hebrews are told to set aside a tithe of their harvest to give thanks to God in a wonderful celebration of Thanksgiving:

> Set apart a tithe of all the yield of your seed that is brought in yearly from the field. In the presence of the Lord your God, in the place that he will choose as a dwelling for his name, you shall eat the tithe of your grain, your wine, and your oil, as well as the firstlings of your herd and flock, so that you may learn to fear the Lord your God always. But if, when the Lord your God has blessed you, the distance is so great that you are unable to transport it, because the place where the Lord your God will choose to set his name is too far away from you, then you may turn it into money. With the money secure in hand, go to the place that the Lord your God will chose; spend the money for whatever you wish—oxen, sheep, wine, strong drink, or whatever you desire. And you shall eat there in the presence of the Lord your God, you and your household rejoicing together. As for the Levites resident in your towns, do not neglect them, because they have no allotment or inheritance with you. Every third year, you shall bring out the full tithe of your produce for that year, and store it within your towns; the Levites, because they have no allotment or inheritance with you, as well as the resident aliens, the orphans, and the widows in your towns, may come and eat their fill so that the Lord your God

may bless you in all the work that you undertake.
–*Deuteronomy 14:22-29*

In Chapter 26, the Hebrews set aside a tithe every third year for the priests, aliens, orphans, and widows, those who are in need:

> When you have finished paying all the tithe of your produce in the third year (which is the year of the tithe), giving it to the Levites, the aliens, the orphans, and the widows, so that they may eat their fill within your towns, then you shall say before the Lord your God: "I have removed the sacred portion from the house, and I have given it to the Levites, the resident aliens, the orphans, and the widows, in accordance with your entire commandment that you commanded me; I have neither transgressed nor forgotten any of your commandments; I have not eaten of it while in mourning; I have not removed any of it while I was unclean; and I have not offered any of it to the dead. I have obeyed the Lord my God, doing just as you commanded me. –*Deuteronomy 26:12-4*

In Malachi, God speaks to the Hebrews in the way of rebuke to those who have not returned their tithe:

> Ever since the days of your ancestors, you have turned aside from my statutes and have not kept them. Return to me, and I will return to you, says the Lord of hosts. But you say, "How shall we return?"
> Will anyone rob God? Yet you are robbing me! But you say, "How are we robbing you?" In your tithes and offerings! You are cursed with a curse, for you are robbing me–the whole nation of you! Bring the full tithe into the storehouse, so that there may be food in my house, and thus put me to the test, says the Lord of hosts; see if will open the windows of heaven for you and pour down for you an overflowing blessing. I will rebuke the locust for you, so that it will not destroy the produce of your soil; and your vine in the field shall not be barren,

says the Lord of hosts. Then all nations will count
you happy, for you will be a land of delight, says the
Lord of hosts. —*Malachi 3:7-12*

In the Hebrew scriptures, wealth was viewed as a sign of
God's blessings and the presentation of tithes was expected as a
sign of our thankfulness for these blessings. Moses, David,
Solomon, and Job were all blessed by God in a material way.
But they were expected to return tithes (10 percent of their
income, produce, wheat, animals, goats, wine, etc.) to care for
the Temple and the poor.

Jesus and Money

In reading the Gospels, it is clear that tithing was the standard of
giving for the Jews at the time of Jesus. Jesus takes tithing for
granted and warns us against making the tithe an idol, about
becoming prideful about it and substituting it for compassion.

But woe to you Pharisees! For you tithe mint and rue
and herbs of all kinds and neglect justice and the
love of God; it is these you ought to have practiced,
without neglecting the others. —*Luke 11:42*

Jesus gave this illustration after observing how much people
were giving at the Temple in Jerusalem. (And you think Jesus
does not care how much we put in the collection plate?)

He looked up and saw rich people putting their gifts
into the treasury; he also saw a poor widow put in
two small copper coins. He said, "Truly I tell you,
this poor widow has put in more than all of them;
for all of them have contributed out of their abundance, but she out of her poverty has put in all she
had to live on. —*Luke 21:1-4*

The widow who gave everything—her offering was held up for
praise. When I have discussed tithing with governing boards,
inevitably someone, usually a man who has a good job and
income, will say: "Remember the widow's mite." I have respond-

ed, "In the New Testament, there is no gift too large in thanksgiving for the kingdom of God. If you want to give all you have, as she did, it will be gratefully accepted." (Obviously, that is not exactly what he had in mind.) As North American Christians, we resemble more the rich giving from our abundance rather than the widow from her scarcity. Overall, I have found widows to be generous in their giving to God through their church. Jesus knows us as we know our own brothers and sisters.

The standard of the widow's mite is observed in monasteries and convents, where, when members accept the life of poverty, chastity, and obedience, they give all their income and assets to the order—truly, "all they have."

Jesus has more to say about us and our possessions (our wealth) than about any other subject of our spiritual life. He tells us:

> Do not be afraid, little flock, for it is your Father's good pleasure to give you the kingdom. Sell your possessions, and give alms. Make purses for yourselves that do not wear out, an unfailing treasure in heaven, where no thief comes near and no moth destroys. For where your treasure is, there your heart will be also. *—Luke 12:32-34*

The value of the kingdom of God requires everything. Our possessions—our house, cars, clothes, and computers—are not going to make it to heaven. We must leave those behind for others. Only *people* are going to heaven. Through the God of materialism, our world tells us to use people to acquire money and wealth to buy things. Jesus calls us to do the opposite: give and invest in our children, our young people, our adults. *Love people and use things!*

Jesus knew well the value of money and the power of wealth. In the parable of the talent (Matthew 25:14-30), a man gives to three servants (slaves) five, two, and one talent each. Jesus is talking about trusting these slaves with real money. For these slaves, "each talent was worth fifteen years of wages as a laborer" (NRSV, Harper Collins). Today, if one is paid the current minimum wage over the course of fifteen years, the equivalent in 1996 dollars would be $132,600. We really should read this passage as: "The master gave to one servant $633,000, to one

$265,200, and to one $132,600." Now that is real money. That gets our attention. The two who doubled their money were told,

> "Well done, good and trustworthy slave; you have been trustworthy in a few things, I will put you in charge of many things; enter into the joy of your master." —*Luke 25:23*

I believe that individually and corporately we are supposed to risk and invest in the kingdom of Heaven. I often see the church not acting as the first two servants did—risking and investing in the kingdom of God—but acting like the third servant, hoarding, afraid it will lose what God has given it.

In the Episcopal church, there is a saying, "When is a business person not a business person? When that person is a member of the vestry." A collorary would be, "When are priests not missionaries? When they preside at a vestry meeting." I have constantly seen business men and women who take risks in business, risks in personal investment, and then, as members of the vestry, act timidly, afraid of risking and using God's money. I have seen clergy who expound great vision, but, when chairing a vestry board meeting, act out of self interest to protect the parish.

Jesus warns us about the power of possession, money, and wealth in the parable of the rich man:

> As he [Jesus] was setting out on a journey, a man ran up and knelt before him, and asked him, "Good teacher, what must I do to inherit eternal life?" Jesus said to him, "Why do you call me good? No one is good but God alone. You know the commandments: 'You shall not murder; You shall not commit adultery; You shall not steal; You shall not bear false witness; You shall not defraud; Honor your father and mother.'" He said to him, "Teacher, I have kept all these since my youth." Jesus, looking at him, loved him and said, "You lack one thing; go, sell what you own, and give the money to the poor, and you will have treasure in heaven; then come, follow me." When he heard this, he was shocked and went away grieving, for he had many possessions. —*Mark 10:17-22*

"Jesus, looking at him, loved him." What a wonderful image of Jesus looking into the man's eyes and loving him and inviting him to be a disciple. All he had to do was sell his possessions and give them to the poor. What an adventure he was offered, life with Jesus. Today, there would be numerous churches named after him—his name would be known along with the names of Peter, Thomas, Mark, and John; instead, he walked away grieving, no name, walking into obscurity with all his possessions, worshiping the God of money and materialism.

It is clear that discipleship requires the commitment of our time, abilities, and money if we are to follow Jesus Christ.

The last scripture I cite concerning the words and teaching of Jesus on money and possessions is from the Gospel According to Matthew:

> No one can serve two masters; for a slave will either hate the one and love the other, or be devoted to the one and despise the other. You cannot serve God and wealth. —*Matthew 6:24*

Each one of us must choose and keep choosing the master we will serve—God or wealth (mammon). In *The Challenge of the Discipline Life*, Richard Foster deals with the power of *mammon*—money. It is not neutral; it has power to control and corrupt the creatures of God. He states:

> What all this talk about stewardship fails to see is that money is not just a neutral medium of exchange but a "power" with a life of its own. And very often it is a "power" that is demonic in character. As long as we think of money in impersonal terms alone, no moral problems exist aside from the proper use of it. But when we begin to take seriously the Biblical perspective that money is animated and energized by "powers" then our relationship to money is filled with moral consequence (page 24).

Our relationship to money is what concerns God. Whom do we worship? What do we worship?

Paul and Money

In 2 Corinthians, Paul tells us about the early church's understanding of money, how it is shared and given to the saints in Jerusalem. He encourages us to be generous:

> The point is this: the one who sows sparingly will also reap sparingly, and the one who sows bountifully will also reap bountifully. Each of you must give as you have made up your mind, not reluctantly or under compulsion, for God loves a cheerful giver. And God is able to provide you with every blessing in abundance, so that by always having enough of everything, you may share abundantly in every good work. —2 Corinthians 9:6-8

We are to give cheerfully out of our abundance, not as the world gives grudgingly out of its scarcity. Thus the early church saw itself abundantly blessed with money, sharing God's blessings of money with the "saints in Jerusalem."

The church's history of stewardship, its use and teachings of our time, abilities and money from the days of Paul and the early church, to Constantine—the age of Christendom, to our time in the nineties—post Christendom, would take a book in itself.

Today we face, as the church and its people have always faced, the power of mammon—money. All around us we are confronted with the God of materialism. A perfect example of this worship of mammon is found in a huge new mall in Towson, Maryland. One walks into this secular cathedral to an atrium four stories high, all open to the ceiling, with waterfalls, sculptures of angels, chairs on which to meditate on the abundance of the God of materialism, classical piano music to inspire the soul, a wonderful dome rivaling St. Peter's in Rome—all this to meet your every need.

- Depressed about your marriage? Buy a new suit—just charge it to your American Express® card.

- Anxious about your job? Buy a pair of designer shoes—just charge them to your Discover® card.

- Afraid of being alone? Buy a 40-inch television with remote control to keep you company. Just charge it to your Visa® card. You won't even have to move from your La-ZBoy® chair to change the 35 channels on your cable.

- Unhappy? Buy a diamond tennis bracelet and charge it to Mastercard®.

- Overweight and slothful? Buy a Nordic® track to bring back your youth. Just write a check and bring your balance down to zero.

The God of materialism has a solution for your every problem. On any Sunday afternoon, it is impossible to find a parking space in the mall's seven-floor parking garage. When was the last time you had to wait for a parking space at church? If a Martian were to look down at Earth, he would indeed see the shopping mall, with its acres of parking lots and hordes of people coming and going in all directions, as our cathedral to the God of money!

The only way we can confront money's power of possessiveness is by giving it away freely and cheerfully, from the wonderful blessings we have received from God.

The words of Jesus still ring in my ears, flash before my eyes and cause my heart to race: "Where your treasure is, there your heart will be also" (Luke 12:34). We need to be vigilant and watchful of our treasure (money). I have acquired a wonderful story that speaks to our earthly and heavenly treasure.

Miss Mary Clark was the wealthiest woman in the small Virginia town of Clarkesville. Never married, she lived alone, in a mansion on top of the highest hill in town.

She attended church occasionally, although she never pledged–she believed in a "freewill offering." Driven by her chauffeur, she attended church every Christmas and Easter. When the plate was passed, she would proudly put her crisp new $100 bill on top of the collection. But that was all she ever gave. When the new church school wing was being built at the church, the Vestry came to her for a major gift; they were trying to raise $200,000 for the project. She knew there were 200 giving units, so, afraid of being taken advantage of, she gave her share of $1,000 and was proud of it. When the new library was being built in town, she gave $100 and was insulted when nothing was named after her. At age 84, God called her home. Her estate of $5 million all went to a distant niece, whom she had last seen 20 years ago and who was married to a heart surgeon.

When she arrived in heaven, St. Peter picked her up in the heavenly bus to take her to her new home. She drove past mansions, which she thought were fitting for a person of her station; she was shocked to see her kind and generous maid, one of the most giving members of her community, living in one of them. The bus kept going, passing through a section of modest houses–one occupied by a teacher from the high school; rowhouses–one occupied by her childhood pastor; and down a dirt road to a ramshackle house with no doors or windows and an unfinished roof. Miss Mary Clark was indignant. In her best upper-class pride, she asked, "What is the meaning of this outrage?" St. Peter responded, "This is the best we could do with what you sent up!"

What are you and the members of your congregation sending up to heaven?

The Episcopal Tithing Story

In the midst of living in a world where, for many, "god" is materialism, where human beings are judged by their yearly income and net worth, the Episcopal church "drew a line in the sand" and took a stand for the Good News of the gospel. In our General Convention of 1982, and at each succeeding General Convention through 1991, they reaffirmed this standard for Episcopalians.

"The tithe is the minimum *standard of giving for God's work."*

This represents a lot of money. It stands in opposition to our world which says, "Accumulate! Hoard! Have!" We say, "Share and give cheerfully to God's work through the church." The tithe is taught not as an absolute, but as a standard. We also teach as a standard that Episcopalians are expected to worship every Sunday, not just when they feel like it or need to.

What is your denomination's standard of giving? If you do not know, do some research. Be able to quote passages and cite sources. If you know in your heart how you feel about giving, look in your checkbook to see how you are practicing it.

There always is the temptation to present the "Lite" church:

- Don't give to God first; just give what's left over at the end of the month.

- Don't give 10 percent. One percent or less is fine.

- Come to church only when you feel like it or it is convenient.

- Keep only eight of the Ten Commandments. Forget the two most troubling ones–your choice.

- Drop the one deadly sin that gives you the most trouble: that will remove the harmful guilt–no need to repent.

- Love only the neighbors you like and those who can be of help to you.

We have wisdom, we are teachable, we can learn what God is calling his servants to be and to give in our time. Our experience tells us that tithing works–it enables us to confront the god of our age–the god of materialism.

Each Sunday, as we gather to worship and serve in Jesus' name, the one minute stewardship sermons communicate the relationship between the mission and vision of the congregation, and the faithful stewardship of each church member and each family's use of time, abilities, and money.

People do not give to meet the budget of the church, but to further the ministry of the parish, the diocese, the world. They do not pledge to pay utility bills (although they realize that these have to be paid), but to provide light and heat in order that we may worship in the church, to assure warm, well-lighted places where children can get to know Jesus, and where community and church groups can meet to learn and be healed. They give so that the sick may be healed, the world may know Jesus–and that they may have a place in which to offer their prayers and receive the sacraments, especially the body and blood of Christ.

Through our teaching and preaching, we can excite our church members about how thankful we are to be invited to be a part of God's plan and work, and how we can return to God a part of what God has given each of us.

I have observed that many of our congregations have members who know how to organize, support, and raise money—lots of money. Our church members constantly work and organize fundraising for the United Way, soccer and little league teams, private and parochial schools, the Democratic and Republican Parties, and myriads of local charities. What is lacking for the church is not organizational skills for fundraising, but a theology of giving—a biblical theology of stewardship. There are wonderful nuts-and-bolts plans on how to conduct an effective stewardship program, but *always* the weak point for our church members is a lack of biblical stewardship theology. This cannot be taught in just one sermon a year, but must be developed slowly, week by week, through repetitive, low-key experiences, like these stewardship sermons.

Too frequently, in our preaching, we focus only on the challenge and commitment of tithing. In *Giving and Stewardship in an Effective Church*, Kennon Callahan defines what motivates people to give and believes that "the grass roots and unchurched" are moved to give by compassion and community, such as are appealed to by these sermons. On a week-to-week basis, they communicate with everyone, the not-yet churched and the grassroots, as well as those who have accepted the challenge and are committed already to tithing.

The stewardship sermons are an important part of my Sunday worship service. Preceding the taking of the offering, I preach one sermon from memory. I believe that the giving of the offering—ourselves—should be a highlight of the service.

I consider this "mini-sermon" as important as the full sermon I share each Sunday with the congregation.

When the offering has been received, we sing the *Doxology* with joy and vigor. We place the offering on the altar and leave it there, as this money given represents what we have received by our time and abilities, and we are returning to God what God has given us. At St. Thomas's Church, money is not treated as evil or worldly, but God's, and I pray out loud that it will be wisely used by our governing board for the building of the kingdom of God.

Money has incredible power to do good or evil. We believe that the power can be harnessed for good–to fulfill Jesus' mission when he speaks of how we will be judged as a person and as a church, as stated in Matthew 25:34-36 (RSV):

> Come, O blessed of my Father, inherit the kingdom prepared for you from the foundation of the world; for I was hungry and you gave me food, I was thirsty and you gave me drink, I was a stranger and you welcomed me, I was naked and you clothed me, I was sick and you visited me, I was in prison and you came to me.

We as clergy and members of Christian communities need to examine our budgets and ministries by Jesus' standards. The money sitting on our altar, freely given, is made sacred to God's work in God's world–to change that world for which Jesus gave his life.

The Right Reverend Charles Longest, Suffragan Bishop of the Episcopal Diocese of Maryland, tells the following story explaining why the offering should be left on the altar.

> A bishop friend of mine, a very good steward himself, and a very good teacher of Christian stewardship, tells this story about an experience he had in a parish in his diocese. As the rubric in the Book of Common Prayer directs, the bishop placed the offering plates on the altar. The acolyte, under audible directions from the rector, started to remove them from the altar. The bishop moved more quickly than the young acolyte and poured the contents of the two plates onto the altar, and went on with the Great Thanksgiving. All that we are and all that we have, we are to return to God in thanksgiving, and it is to be "placed on the altar"–the altar of God's love and God's self-giving and God's creation and re-creation. This *total offering* of "our souls and bodies" is placed on the altar of Thanksgiving. God accepts it; God takes it; God blesses it; God gives it back to us– healed, restored, forgiven, and strengthened for God's service.

HOW TO CONSTRUCT ONE MINUTE STEWARDSHIP SERMONS

Section II

SECTION II
How to Construct One Minute Stewardship Sermons

MY EXPERIENCE HAS LED ME TO BELIEVE that a stewardship sermon from every pastor of every church every Sunday would significantly aid our members to understand what their church is accomplishing through their giving of their time, abilities, and money. Surely, this would inspire increased giving to fulfill the mission of the church.

Gather together the stewardship committee of your church and at a vestry meeting, make a list of exactly what the Sunday offering–your members' giving of time, abilities, and money–is accomplishing through your church. Do not limit this list to your own church ministries alone, but also include what the offering accomplishes in the community and the larger church in the name of Jesus Christ. My experience has taught me that this experience is a satisfying one for the stewardship committee, the members of the vestry, and the clergy, all of whom will feel a sense of accomplishment and well-being when they see clearly exactly what their church is doing with its ministry.

Keep this list and check off from it each Sunday's accomplishments. Then thank your congregation.

Each Sunday, I focus on a verse from Scripture or a special day in the church year, such as Palm Sunday, or an event in the life of our church, such as the opening of church school. Turning to the Cross References in the back of this book, read the appropriate sermons for inspiration and examples. Memorize one of these or construct your own. Suppose, for example, the weekly Scripture is Hebrews 13:16:

> Do not neglect to do good and to share what you
> have for such sacrifices are pleasing to God.

In the Cross Reference, you will find that Hebrews 13:16 is covered in G-9 (p. 27): Read the two Sermons; copy one and type it out or revise it in your own words. Then share it at the Offertory.

Another example: If next Sunday is Palm Sunday, you will find it listed in the Sermons for the Church Year and cross-referenced under Scripture (CY-9, pages 45-46). Memorize one of these sermons or write one of our own perhaps using Matthew 21:1-11; Mark 11:1-11; or Luke 19:29-46.

You might also use an event in the life of Christ or an event in the life of your own church. By using these one minute sermons, you will be thanking your people for giving their time, abilities, and money to enable your church to accomplish its mission—and to make it possible to worship and serve in the name of Jesus.

ONE
MINUTE
STEWARDSHIP
SERMONS

Section III

—— G-1 ——

In many churches, clergy exhort their parishioners to "give until it hurts." All we have found is that [*insert your denomination*] have a "very low pain threshold." I hope we will give until it feels *good*. The money we give each week enables [*St. Thomas's*] to be a giving, godly force in our community and our world.

When we make our special offering this morning for [*St. Thomas's Church*], how do you think God will feel? Will God respond with "That was wonderful. You really shouldn't have done it. Your generosity pleases me. Thank you for your generous gift." I believe God *does* care. Please be generous.

—— G-2 ——

Offer to God a sacrifice of thanksgiving, and make good your vows to the Most High.
> *Psalm 50:14*
> *Book of Common Prayer, page 376*

Is the offering in your envelope today a sacrifice of thanksgiving? Is it a true sacrifice for you and your family? Is it given in thanksgiving? We here at [*St. Thomas's*] believe that all we have and all our time, ability, and money are gifts from a glorious and generous God. Today, we are thankfully offering back to God only a part of that which God has given us. I thank you for your faithfulness in your giving.

This morning, at this time, we will take up a collection in the offertory plates. We do this every service at [*St. Thomas's*]. The Psalmist tells us to do this in a spirit of sacrifice and thanksgiving. Sacrifice means that the gift we offer makes a difference in our lives. I thank God for the sacrifices you are making every week in thanksgiving for the way that God has blessed you.

—— G-3 ——

I appeal to you, therefore, brothers and sisters, by the mercies of God, to present your bodies as a living sacrifice, holy and acceptable to God, which is your spiritual worship.
> *Romans 12:1*

When we come to church, we offer God three things: our *time*—an hour and a half—of our *talents*—our abilities to pray, praise, sing, worship—and our *money*. God accepts these, because God wants not our gifts, but us as Givers. God wants us. We are the living sacrifice.

Did you prepare yourselves today to be a living sacrifice to God? What kind of sacrifice does God want? How is your stewardship of God's creation sacrificed? Each Sunday, we present ourselves at God's altar—we pray for God's mercy that we and our gifts are acceptable.

—— G-4 ——

Ascribe to the Lord the honor due His name; bring offering and come in to His courts.
> *Psalm 96:8*
> *Book of Common Prayer, page 373*

Each week as you write your check or put your money in your offering envelope, you are making a spiritual act of thanksgiving for all of God's gifts. It is an act of graciousness, of appreciation for God's work throughout our daily lives. Please be generous, for we are returning to God a portion of what God has given us.

∽

Each week, we gather to praise God through our worship of one God (the Father, Creator; the Son, Redeemer; and the Holy Spirit, Our Sanctifier). We know God when we bring our offerings to the altar. They symbolize our stewardship—the management of our time, abilities, and money, that which we return to God through God's church to proclaim God's kingdom. Thank you for your generosity.

—— G-5 ——

You are worthy, our Lord and God, to receive glory and honor and power; for you have created all things, and by your will, they existed and were created.
Revelation 4:11

∽

God is the author of our creation. God created the world and God created us. Often, I hear someone say, "I am a self-made man (or woman)." Such people worship themselves as their own creator. This morning we acknowledge the Lord, our Father—our Creator. We worship not ourselves, but God, who created us. Our stewardship of time, abilities, and money acknowledges that God created all of us.

∽

This morning, through our worship, we offer God our glory, honor, and power. Our offerings this morning of our time, ability, and money are the grateful response of the created, returning to the Creator a gift of God's creation. Through your generous gifts, we here at [*St. Thomas's*] proclaim the Creator to the world.

——— G-6 ———

Ascribe to the Lord the honor due His name; bring offerings and come into His courts.
Psalm 96:8
Book of Common Prayer, page 376

Your offering envelopes this morning honor our God. Our gifts let God know in a very tangible way how much we honor the name, the person, the courts, and this house–a very holy place– made holy by the presence of God this morning. We will place our gifts to God on the altar to be blessed and used for God's work in God's church and God's world. I give thanks that you are here this morning to present your offering.

This morning, we are bringing our offerings to our Lord, God. We are honoring God's name at [*St. Thomas's*]. We are in God's place, the courts where we gather each week to worship God, to know Jesus, to be guided by the Holy Spirit. I give thanks to all who have brought their offerings this morning. Your offerings will enable [*St. Thomas' s*] to continue to proclaim the Word of God and to be God's church in this holy place.

—— G-7 ——

Walk in love, as Christ loved us and gave Himself for us, an offering and sacrifice to God.

Ephesians 5:2
Book of Common Prayer, page 343

Paul tells us to walk in love with Jesus, as Jesus loves us. Jesus died on the cross, because he loves us that much. Our offerings this morning are given in love, in response to the love of Jesus for us. Thank you for your offerings–a living, tangible way of saying, "Jesus, we love you."

Is your offering a sacrifice to God? Jesus gave himself on the cross for us. This morning, we offer ourselves in thanksgiving for Jesus Christ's love for us. It is our sacrifice that the church here, [*insert the name of your church, the regional body, such as the Diocese of Maryland, and our national church*] can proclaim the love of Jesus Christ.

—— G-8 ——

So when you are offering your gift at the altar, if you remember that your brother or sister has something against you, leave your gift there before the altar and go; first be reconciled to your brother or sister, and then come and offer your gift.

Matthew 5:23-24

This morning's offering relates the gift of money we bring to the altar for others. If you are alienated from your mother or father, your brother or sister, friend, neighbor, or co-worker, make peace with that person today. Be reconciled that your stewardship of time, ability, and money will be acceptable to God.

∽

This morning, as we present ourselves as an offering to God, if you are alienated from a family member, today may be the day to telephone or visit or write a note to heal that wound and bring about reconciliation. We offer our time, abilities, and money this morning in thanksgiving for God's reconciling love for each of us.

⸺ G-9 ⸺

Do not neglect to do good and to share what you have, for such sacrifices are pleasing to God.
Hebrews 13:16

∽

We are called upon to do good—"To worship and serve in Jesus' name." We always need to remember that Jesus died for the world and not for the church. Your offering this morning will be shared and do good in the world caring for God's children. Thank you.

∽

As children, we are born selfish. The first words most children learn after *Mommy* and *Daddy* are *my* and *mine*. As followers of the way of Jesus, we learn to share and to do good. Through our stewardship—the giving of our time, abilities, and money—we break this guise of selfishness. *Me* and *mine* become *ours*. We give to do God's work in the world. Thank you for your generous gifts this morning to do God's work.

—— G-10 ——

Let us with gladness present the offerings and oblations of our life and labor to the Lord.
Book of Common Prayer, page 377

∞

This morning, we will joyfully present our offerings of money to the Lord; but we will offer not just our money, we will present our oblations, the bread and wine, which will be consecrated and then given to us as the body and blood of Christ. The money, the bread, and the wine will all be placed on the altar representing us and who we are (our thankfulness to God and our love of Jesus Christ).

∞

According to the Psalmist, our offerings, the money we joyfully give this morning, represent to God our life and labor. Our oblations, the bread and wine, symbolize all of God's gifts to us. Together, they represent our labor, our time and ability(the work for which we are paid). However, God doesn't want just our gifts of money, God wants the givers–us. I thank God you chose to be here this morning to offer your gifts and yourselves joyfully to God. I thank you for coming to share joyfully with me this Holy Eucharist–Great Thanksgiving!

—— G-11 ——

Open, O Lord, the eyes of all people to behold thy gracious hand in all thy works, that, rejoicing in thy whole creation, they may honor thee with their substance and be faithful stewards of thy bounty.
Book of Common Prayer, page 329

∞

Today we rejoice in God's creation. To be a Christian is to be an ecologist, for we acknowledge that God has given us care and stewardship over God's creation and we are accountable. I pray each of us will be faithful stewards.

∞

Today in our prayers, Christians are, by our very theology, ecologists. We love this planet Earth that God has created for us. What we return, comes from God. With our offering this morning, we honor God. Thank you.

—— G-12 ——

For the just and proper use of your creation.
Book of Common Prayer, page 392

∞

This morning, I would like to have us think about the stewardship of God's creation. The ecological movement has been raising our consciousness about our endangered earth. God has given us stewardship and management of all creation, and we have littered, polluted, and destroyed it. I believe that Christians need to provide the leadership for a reverence and care of God's creation. We need to capture the sense of the Hebrew Bible that we must care for our children's children by our stewardship of God's earth today.

∞

What do you think God thinks about the way we have cared for and used God's creation? Are we treating it lovingly with the tender care it deserves or are we polluting it and destroying it little by little? God has given us stewardship over all creation. At our death, we will be called home to God and I believe we will all be held accountable for the earth we have left for our children's children. I pray that as we practice good stewardship of our time, abilities, and money, we will practice good stewardship of the earth as well.

—— G-13 ——

For the good earth which God has given us, and for the wisdom and will to conserve it, let us pray to the Lord.
Book of Common Prayer, page 384

Today we thanked God for our earth(our planet). We also prayed for the good sense to care for it as good stewards. By nature, Christians are ecologists. We know God created our earth and saw that it was good. As we practice our personal stewardship, remember: we are accountable to our children and our children's children for the earth we leave them.

[*Begin with a personalized description of fall in a beautiful local spot in or near your community.*] The leaves are changing colors. The water is crystal blue. What a glorious portrait of God's Beauty and Creation! I pray that each of us, as part of our stewardship, will conserve this beauty. Our Sunday offering is one way that we thank God for God's creation. Thank you for sharing in this offering of our thanks.

—— G-14 ——

Give us a reverence for the earth as Your own creation, that we may use its resources rightly in the service of others and to Your honor and glory.
Book of Common Prayer, page 388

Do we have a reverence for the earth as God's creation or do we think of it as a planet to be exploited? Do we use the earth's resources to serve others or only for our own comforts? These questions of stewardship define how we are honoring God. Stewardship is not just the use of our time, abilities, and money for our local church, but good stewardship is how we care for all of God's world and people. I thank you for being here this morning, as we gather together to thank God for God's creation.

We are held accountable for how we treat this planet Earth, and how we love, care for, and serve others. It is a "both-and" love for God's creation and for God's children. I thank God that you are here this Sunday as we reverently thank God for God's creation and return to God what has been given to us: our time, our abilities, and our money to be used for the service of others.

—— G-15 ——

For a blessing upon all human labor, and for the right use of the riches of creation, that the world may be freed from poverty, famine, and disaster, we pray to you, O Lord.
Book of Common Prayer, page 390

This morning, we prayed "for a blessing upon all human labor and for the right use of the riches of creation." Our offering, the money we place in the collection plates, represents our human labor, our use of our time and our abilities, for which we have been paid. This morning, we will place this offering on the altar to be blessed by God for God's work through this church and throughout this diocese. We pray that these offerings will be used wisely. Thank you for your faithful offerings each week.

When the collection is taken this morning, we will place the collection plates on the altar. We will sing the *Doxology* and say thank you for all of God's blessings upon us. We will then bless this offering and pray that our governing board will use the money rightly and wisely for the building up of God's kingdom and caring for those suffering from poverty, famine, and disaster. I give thanks for your trust in this church–that we will use the money you give to continue God's work.

—— G-16 ——

"It is easier for a camel to go through the eye of a needle than for someone who is rich to enter the kingdom of God."
Mark 10:25

∞

Jesus' whimsical illustration of a camel trying to pass through the eye of a needle certainly does not mean that it is impossible for the wealthy to enter into God's kingdom. It *does* mean that when the piling up of riches becomes an end in itself, rather than a means toward an end, that is debilitating. The rich man's understanding of stewardship is all-important here. Love must be directed toward God and people who can return love, and not toward wealth, which cannot.

Canon David W. Crockett
Episcopal Diocese of Western Massachusetts

—— G-17 ——

Jesus answered, "My kingdom is not from the world."
John 18:36

∞

Jesus made it amply clear that His kingdom was not of this world. It is neither temporal nor political, but rather is of the spiritual realm. As inheritors of the kingdom of heaven, Christians are in this world, but not of it, and therefore must exercise extraordinary care where we place our allegiances. When we rely on property, possessions, material objects, and wealth, we make "things" our sovereign and place our trust in them rather than in the King of kings. Stewardship helps us to put first things first.

Canon David W. Crockett
Episcopal Diocese of Western Massachusetts

———— G-18 ————

Matthew 25:31-46

Jesus' story of the Last Judgment tells us of our duty and responsibilities toward the least of our brothers and sisters. Unhappily, the hungry, naked, thirsty, sick, and imprisoned represent the majority of humankind. Our part in the war against hunger and poverty begins with our Christian commitment. You and I are called upon to minister to all peoples and dare not "ignore the least of these."

Canon David W. Crockett
Episcopal Diocese of Western Massachusetts

———— G-19 ————

Greed

Therefore, since we are surrounded by so great a cloud of witnesses, let us also lay aside every weight and the sin that clings so closely, and let us run with perseverance the race that is set before us.
Hebrews 12:1

I want you to close your eyes and imagine that you have suddenly been transported back in time more than fifty years ago, to the year 1946. In your mind's eye, see the persons in the pew in front of you. The man is wearing a uniform, with hash marks on the sleeve. He has just returned from Europe where he served in the infantry. Next to him is his young wife, wearing a red that with a jaunty feather. The Offertory Sentence is spoken. He reaches into his back pocket to pull out his wallet. Carefully, he removes a folded ten dollar bill and places it in the offering plate. He is grateful to God for his homecoming to this church where he was baptized twenty-two years before. He bows his head in thanksgiving. Over the many years since, he has put thousands of dollars in that same plate, Sunday by Sunday, as witness to his faith and gratitude. He is here in spirit now, in the pew where he always sat, in his beloved church, and many more are here with him. You are surrounded by a great cloud of unseen witnesses who have given so much. It is now your turn—make your witness in giving so that others will follow you.

The Rev. Roy W. Cole
Interim Specialist for Revitalization

What is the sin that clings so closely to each and every one of us? Simply put, it is greed. We are a greedy people. We live in a greedy culture that places material goods and access to them as a supreme value. It makes us a greedy people and greed is a sin—in our culture, it is a sin that clings very closely to each one of us—every day—and will, unless we decide to do something about it. The remedy for greed is giving. Greedy people need to give to get over their greed and become spiritually healthy. This morning, do something for yourself. Give and give generously until that nervous feeling induced by greed gives away to joy(which is what you feel when you are delivered from a sin that clings so, so closely.

The Rev. Roy W. Cole
Interim Specialist for Revitalization

--- G-20 ---

Giving

Therefore, since we are surrounded by so great a cloud of witnesses, let us lay aside every weight and the sin that clings so closely, and let us run with perseverance the race that is set before us.
Hebrews 12:1

∞

I want you to think back to a time when you were a kid and as all kids do, you got into a race. Maybe it was in school, maybe it was with a close friend or your brother or sister. Do you remember running as fast as you could with somebody gaining on you? Your breath is coming hard, yet you keep on running. A pain starts up in your side, yet the sheer exhilaration of the race keeps you going. At the finish line, you collapse on the grass You won! Yes, you won! What joy! Giving is like that—the strange combination of effort, a painful stretching of yourself, leading to joy. Give till you feel the joy. Run the race set before you. Make a difference!

The Rev. Roy W. Cole
Interim Specialist for Revitalization

--- G-21 ---

Giving

You will be enriched in every way for your great generosity, which will produce thanksgiving to God.
2 Corinthians 9:11

∞

It was a bone-chilling day; the soup line moved slowly. The young woman blew on her fingers and stamped her feet as the line shuffled along. Finally, she was inside the door. Warmth and the wonderful smell of good soup and fresh bread lifted her spirits. As her gaze swept the room, her eyes fell on a sign, a small hand-written sign: "You are welcome, you are the guest of Christ." She bowed her head and gave thanks to this unknown one called Christ. Give so that others may give thanks to the One from whom all gifts flow.

The Rev. Roy W. Cole
Interim Specialist for Revitalization

—— G-22 ——

Giving

Remembering the words of the Lord Jesus, for he himself said, "It is more blessed to give than to receive."
Acts 20:35

I know of a couple who gathered a church of homeless people in Las Vegas, Nevada, a town not known for its generosity to the poor. Each Sunday, in this little church, the offertory plate was passed with the words, "Give as you are able; take from it if you are in need." Each Sunday, the plate was filled with dimes, quarters, and sometimes, a crumpled bill. No one took from the plate as it was passed. Each Sunday, the congregation chose one of their own—the most needy—to receive the offering. In their giving of what little they had, they were blessed and were a blessing to one of their own. A mother of a sick child, who was given the offering one Sunday, wiped tears from her eyes as she said that no one had ever just given her money before. Thank you, God. It is truly more blessed to give than to receive.

The Rev. Roy W. Cole
Interim Specialist for Revitalization

— G-23 —

Choices

"No one can serve two masters; for a slave will either hate the one and love the other, or be devoted to the one and despise the other. You cannot serve God and wealth."
Matthew 6:24

The folklore of all peoples is filled with stories of fateful choices: persons finding themselves before two doors—one door leading to disaster, one to untold bliss. To avoid forks in the road like that Robert Frost paints in his famous poem which describes a crossroad illustrates a truth that our lives are determined forever by the choices we make. Week after week, we are offered a choice to declare ourselves to others and to our God, as to whom we belong—the small god Mammon or the great God whom Jesus called ABBA, Father. Choose wisely. Give to God that which God is due of the first fruits of your wealth.

The Rev. Roy W. Cole
Interim Specialist for Revitalization

— CY-1 —

Advent Sunday (First Sunday of Advent)
Matthew 24:37-44 Mark 13:33-37 Luke 21:25-31

For many Christians, this Sunday marks the beginning of our Church Year. It is a season of expectation and preparation for the birth of Jesus Christ.

∞

Today is the first Sunday of Advent–the New Year. It is a time we prepare our hearts and souls for the coming birth of Christ. It is a time of expectation, of watchfulness, and a time of self-examination. We examine our stewardship of time, abilities, and money and consider how we are using all three for the proclaiming of God's kingdom. Thank you for your offering today. It will go toward building God's kingdom.

∞

Happy New Year! Today we begin a new year at [*St. Thomas's Church*]. We are preparing with expectation for the birth of Jesus on December 25. We are told by the world around us to buy, buy, buy to show our love for our loved ones. We are told by the world to use money we do not have, to buy things we do not need, to impress people we do not even like. Our gifts given at church each week show our appreciation for God's love for us. It is our gift, given to God weekly. Thank you for your stewardship that enables us to proclaim the Son of God, Jesus!

— CY-2 —

Advent (Fourth Sunday)
Matthew 1:18-25 Luke 1:26-38 Luke 1:39-49

This fourth Sunday of Advent has become Mary's Sunday in the Episcopal Church. We have lit the pink candle in our Advent wreath to honor Mary, Mother of Jesus. Mary said *Yes* to God. Each Sunday, when we make our offerings, we, too, are saying Yes to God—our response in love and compassion to the gift of Jesus Christ. Thank you for your generous gifts.

ⓧ

Today, we remember Mary and Joseph. Joseph is known as the patron saint of stepfathers. He accepted, loved, and taught Jesus as his own son. All that we have is a gift from God. When we love and care for our spouse and children, we are doing God's work. Thank you for your faithful offerings. They are one way we take care of God's family.

— CY-3 —

Epiphany (The Coming of the Wise Men)
Matthew 2:1-12

Today, we remember the coming of the Wise Men to the baby Jesus in Bethlehem. They brought with them their gifts of gold, frankincense, and myrrh. This morning, we brought with us our parish envelope as our gift to the Christ Child, to pay Him homage. We do this each time we gather together. We, like the Wise Men, bring our gifts to honor our Lord and Savior. Thank you for your generous gifts. You are enabling [*St. Thomas's*] to tell the story.

ⓧ

Wise men and wise women still seek Him! The Wise Men jour-
neyed from the East to find the Christ Child, Jesus. We have trav-
eled to [*St. Thomas's*] this morning seeking Jesus and we have
brought our gifts that represent gold, frankincense, and myrrh. Our
offering this morning is ourselves–our time, abilities, and money.
By our gifts, we are making Jesus known throughout our world.

―― CY-4 ――

Baptism Of Jesus (First Sunday After Epiphany)
Matthew 3:13-17 Mark 1:7-11 Luke 3:15-16; 21-22

Today we remember the baptism of Jesus Christ in the River
Jordan, by John the Baptist. In all of the accounts from Matthew,
Mark and Luke, God proclaims from Heaven words such as:
"This is my Son, the Beloved, with whom I am well pleased." This
affirmation begins the ministry of Jesus. In our own baptism, we
begin our ministry , our stewardship of time, abilities, and money.
I give thanks for your stewardship-ministry at [*St. Thomas's*].

☙

The baptism of Jesus by John at the River Jordan begins Christ's
ministry. I pray that each of us in our own ministry and stewardship hears the words of God: "You are my child, beloved,
with whom I am well pleased." I thank our Father for your faithful stewardship of time, abilities, and money. You are enabling us
"to worship and serve in Jesus' name."

☙

―― CY-5 ――

Transfiguration (The Last Sunday Of Epiphany)
Matthew 17:1-9 Mark 9:2-9 Luke 9:28-35

When Jesus goes to the mountain with Peter, James, and John, He
is transfigured. The Episcopal Book of Common Prayer celebrates
this transfiguration on August 6 and the last Sunday of Epiphany.

☙

Today we remember the Transfiguration. Jesus is transfigured by God, and God speaks: "This is my Son, the Beloved; listen to him!" (Mark 9: 2-9). We are called to listen to Jesus, and by his teaching, we live our lives as children of God. Jesus lived his life intimately with the disciples. We too are called upon, as part of our stewardship, to live our lives with love and compassion with those whom God has given us. Your generous offerings help us to live and proclaim God's love at [*St. Thomas's*].

∞

The Transfiguration is one of the great feasts of the Christian year. God proclaims to Jesus and to the disciples: "This is my Son, my Chosen; listen to him!" (Luke 9:35). Jesus is affirmed by God. Each Sunday, we at [*St. Thomas's*] are affirmed as beloved children of God. Your generous gifts of time, ability, and money make this affirmation possible. Thank you.

———— CY-6 ————

Ash Wednesday
Joel 2:1-2 Matthew 6:1-6; 16-21

In the Christian tradition, Ash Wednesday is the first day of Lent. In most liturgical churches, ashes are made available to those who choose to receive them.

∞

Jesus tells us that when we give, it should be done in secret. That is one reason for our church envelopes–what you give should be known only to God. God cares about what we do. Today we have received ashes symbolizing our mortality and penitence. "Remember that you are dust, and to dust you shall return" (*The Book of Common Prayer* page 265). Remember, too, the old Jewish saying: "There are no pockets in the shroud!"

∞

Today we remember our mortality and penitence; it is a time for self examination. We have repented of "our intemperate love of worldly goods and comforts" (*The Book of Common Prayer* page 268). Each time we make our gifts at the offering, we are affirming a new way of godly life. I thank you for our repentance and faith this night (day).

— CY-7 —

The First Sunday of Lent

Today, Jesus is tempted. We are often tempted not to live up to our highest potential as children of God. Like Jesus, our temptations may not be so much to do evil as to choose some lesser good. Often we do this with our giving. We choose to be less giving than we know we could be, less generous than we think we should be. Subtly, the devil tempts us to think that our gift is sufficient. Lent is a time for reminding us that the Lord calls us to the highest form of discipleship and the most challenging aspects of giving. Lent calls us to be more generous and to take hold of life to its fullest.

The Rt. Rev. Robert Ihloff
Episcopal Bishop of Maryland

For forty days, Jesus took stock of his life—who he was and what he wanted to accomplish. We call this forty-day period Lent. Christians are called in Lent to a special period of taking stock, of setting priorities, of rethinking what it means to be a steward of God's gift. May this holy season be a time for you to contemplate anew the many blessings of God and to respond to God by a generous giving of your very selves. Generous giving always brings rewards, as our Lord found out. And while generous giving does not protect us from the difficulties and vagaries of life, it does assure us of a deeper life. As surely as Lent ends with Easter, so a life of giving ends with a greater sense of satisfaction and greater joy.

The Rt. Rev. Robert Ihloff
Episcopal Bishop of Maryland

—— CY-8 ——

Mothering Sunday (The Fourth Sunday of Lent)

In the Anglican Church of England, the fourth Sunday of Lent–Refreshment Sunday–is called Mothering Sunday. In the past, unmarried girls working as maids would be given the day off to return home to be with their mothers. On their way home, the young girls would pick wild flowers to take to their mothers and mothers would bake a special simnel cake. At St. Thomas', we celebrate this day in a very special way. The clergy buy simple carnations to be pinned on all women, and after both the 8:00 a.m. and the 10:00 a.m. service, we have a special reception to honor all these women (they mother our church!).

This morning all of our ladies received a corsage in honor of the women of [*St. Thomas's*]. Every woman is a mother here–you are called upon to care for our children, who through their baptism have been adopted by grace and by our congregation. We men appreciate the way you give lovingly of your stewardship of time, ability, and money to God through our church. Following our service this morning, we will have a reception in your honor. Thank you for your gifts.

It is wonderful to have so many "mothers" here today. We honor all of the faithful women of our parish–our mothers in the family of God. Your corsages are our thanks for all that you do. It is part of our stewardship. I thank the entire congregation for your generous weekly giving to God through His church. We are working to become a more loving and forgiving community.

—— CY-9 ——

Palm Sunday (Liturgy of the Palms)
Matthew 21:1-11 Mark 11:1-11A Luke 19: 29-49

Today, we remember Jesus' entrance into Jerusalem. He comes from the village of Bethany riding on a donkey and is proclaimed the Messiah: "Hosanna to the Son of David! Blessed is the one who comes in the name of the Lord! Hosanna in the highest heaven!" As part of his stewardship, a poor villager has provided the donkey for Jesus' ride. In such a small, yet significant way, we, too, provide for the ministry of Christ. May we in our own stewardship be as faithful as this unnamed villager.

Today, we have re-enacted the coming of Jesus into Jerusalem. We have blessed the palms and held them as we proclaimed Jesus as "The One!" Those in Jerusalem used the palms to wave and cover the road. Those who honored Jesus, then, used palms; today, we honor him in our own way as we proclaim him our Lord and Savior. Our gifts, generously given this day, enable [St. Thomas's] to proclaim this Holy Week the wonderful story of God's redemption for humankind.

Today is a day of jarring contrast. We have welcomed Jesus into Jerusalem, but we have also participated in the story of his crucifixion. In a short period of time those who have sung his praises turn against Jesus and cry out, "Crucify him!" This contrast says something sobering about human nature. It is easy to give lip service or even to become excited about something new. When we discover that it may cost us, especially if that cost is personal or dear, it may be much more difficult to keep our enthusiasm. Serving God as a steward requires that we really give of ourselves for the long term. God calls us to respond with more than lip service. True discipleship manifests itself in giving our all–giving of our time, our talents, and our resources–that the work of God can be done and the blessings we have can be shared.

The Rt. Rev. Robert Ihloff
Episcopal Bishop of Maryland

We welcome Jesus this day as our Lord and Savior. It is easy to be enthusiastic, even to be carried away briefly with that enthusiasm. It is much harder to sustain enthusiasm, because that means giving of ourselves. Is it any wonder that many who welcomed Jesus in Jerusalem fell away in their enthusiasm or even turned against him? The Lord gave his all. In so doing, he invites us to be more generous, to give of our very selves that the ministry of love and reconciliation may spread throughout the world. At the beginning of this holiest week, let us pledge ourselves to be more generous, to be more giving. And let us pray that our enthusiasm may not wane, but remain strong for the glory of God and the welfare of our community.

The Rt. Rev. Robert Ihloff
Episcopal Bishop of Maryland

—— CY-10 ——

Maundy Thursday
John 13:1-15 Luke 22:14-30

Today, we remember the Institution of the Eucharist [from Luke] or in John, the Great Commandment and the Washing of the Feet.

∞

Tonight, we remember the time Jesus instituted the Eucharist and shared with his disciples the Passion meal in a new way that would change our world forever. Tonight, when the bread and wine are presented, think of that first time. Jesus will be betrayed and fastened to the cross tomorrow. At this moment, we say, "Thank you." I say thank you for all the wonderful gifts you give of yourselves to God at God's altar tonight and at every Eucharist.

∞

In the Gospel of John, Jesus demonstrates what it means to love one another by washing the feet of his disciples. Jesus practiced His stewardship by example. Tomorrow, he will give his life for us, so that we will have no doubt just how much he and God love us. Tonight, our offerings of time, abilities, and money are given in response to his love for us. I thank you for being here tonight, as we share together this time with Jesus.

—— CY-11 ——

Good Friday
John 13:1-15 Luke 22:14-30

Today's offering is sent to the church in Jerusalem for the work of Jesus Christ in that part of the world. Like Paul, we remember the Christians in Jerusalem.

∞

Today we remember the ultimate sacrifice of Jesus on the cross. As an act of his ultimate stewardship, he gave all that He had— gave his very life for us, to remove any doubts we might have about how much we are loved by God. The offering we give today is for the first church founded in Jerusalem. I have seen the work being done in the Holy Land by this church, even under persecution, and how it is witnessing to the resurrection of Jesus Christ in a hostile world. I ask you to be generous.

Today is Good Friday. It is called "good" because on this day, Christ died for us that we would know eternal life. Tonight, our Good Friday offering goes to the first church founded in Jerusalem as a witness to our faith. It is part of our stewardship of money here at [*St. Thomas's*]. I have seen the godly work this church in Jerusalem is doing under extremely hostile and difficult conditions. I thank you for your generous response.

—— CY-12 ——

Easter Sunday
Matthew 28:1-10 Mark 16:1-8 Luke 24:1-10 John 20:1-10

Today, we gather to celebrate the resurrection of Jesus Christ. We have sung wonderful hymns that speak of our praise, adoration, and joy! But in reality, every Sunday in the Christian Church is an Easter Sunday, because we remember Christ's resurrection each week. I thank you for your generous weekly offerings, your stewardship of your time, your ability, and your money. They make it possible for [*St. Thomas's Church*] to be able to preach the Easter message every day.

It is a wonderful day for the church of Jesus Christ as the faithful members of his congregation gather to worship him on the day of his resurrection Throughout the world, the message of his triumph over death and Good Friday is being told. I am thankful that God has brought us together at [*St. Thomas's*] to rejoice and praise Jesus and to share in his Holy Eucharist. We offer ourselves this morning—our time, our abilities, and our money—for the telling of the story, so that at [*St. Thomas's*] and throughout the world, Jesus will be made known. Thank you!

—— CY-13 ——

Pentecost
Acts 2:1-11

We celebrate Pentecost as part of the three days that changed our lives forever—Christmas, Easter, and Pentecost. At St. Thomas's, we request that all parishioners wear something red to remind us of the Holy Spirit. We have a special chasuble made by the Altar Guild from a bed sheet and laid on a table. Each person who comes in is asked to write a message on it to God and sign it with red ink for me to wear during the service. On this day, I literally "wear the church," and this symbolizes that the church is not a building, but the gathered people of God. At our Hospitality Hour, we have a huge sheet cake celebrating the birthday of the church. (Normally, our church is overflowing on this day.)

Thank you for being here with the family of [*St. Thomas's*] to celebrate Pentecost today. It is wonderful to see a sea of red, as we acknowledge the Holy Spirit who inspires our worship and our faith, and gives us the power, week by week, to proclaim the kingdom of God. I wear this chasuble, signed by all of you, to symbolize that we are all the Church—it is not a building, but the people of God gathered together today. Thank you for your faithful stewardship of time, ability, and money that enables us to be the church.

Today is a day in the life of our church equal to Christmas and Easter. The first Pentecost, when the Holy Spirit came upon the disciples, three thousand were baptized by the Holy Spirit. Today is the church's birthday, and for children of all ages, we will have a huge birthday cake at our Hospitality Hour. When you go to a birthday party, you always bring a gift. Today, we bring our gifts to the church to celebrate its birth. Thank you for your generous offering this morning. By your gifts, we are building the church.

――― CY-14 ―――

Last Sunday After Pentecost
Matthew 25:31-46

The Least of These

Jesus' story of the Last Judgment tells us of our duty and responsibilities to "the least of these my brethren." Truly, it is *most* of God's children and our brethren, not the *least* of them who are hungry, naked, thirsty, sick, and imprisoned. They are the majority of humankind, representing somewhere between one-half and two-thirds of *God's* children. "The least of these" are being consumed with the struggle for mere survival.

☙

The word *least* might refer to our attitudes and understanding of the needs of the hungry and naked peoples of this world, who are nearby as well as far off. What does Jesus have to say about our position in life among the "haves" when there are so many "have-nots"? What are our attitudes about the desperate in this world? Can we as Christians close our hearts to them? Surely, we cannot.

Our part in the war against hunger and poverty begins and ends with our Christian commitment or lack of the same. We are called upon to be good stewards of God's many gifts. We are to conserve, protect, and husband the resources of his world as a beginning, but our Christian responsibility calls out to us:

To do good, and distribute, forget not;
for with such sacrifices God is well pleased.
Hebrews 13:16
The Book Of Common Prayer

☙

We who are called upon to minister to all peoples dare not be content and ignore "the least of these."

Canon David W. Crockett
Episcopal Diocese of Western Massachusetts

—— CY-15 ——

All Saints' Day
Matthew 5:1-12

At our All Saints' service, we remember by name all those who have been buried from [*St. Thomas's*] during the past year. We also mention all of those who have asked to be remembered on a sign-up list in the entryway to the church. In addition, I send a personal letter to the families of all who have been buried this past year and we invite them to be present as we remember their loved ones by name.

Today, we have remembered by name all who have died, and we pray that through God's mercy, our loved ones are now with God in Paradise. We appreciate their past stewardship. By their sharing of their time, abilities, and money, [*St. Thomas*] stands here, a holy place on a hill. By example, they have taught us what it means to be a loving, caring Christian, committed to doing God's work through this church.

This morning, we give thanks for all of those we have remembered by name, who we pray are now in God's kingdom. We appreciate all that they have done through their lives to practice good stewardship of their time, abilities, and money to have made [*St. Thomas's*] the church that it is today. I pray that through our stewardship, we can continue to "worship and serve in Jesus' name."

On this day, we remember all those who have come before us in our families, in our parish, and in our community. We are part of an intricate web of relationships with many people. These saints remain among us in our inheritances. In our parish, look around and see what the legacies are in our worship, ministries, and physical surroundings. In our personal lives, we are a part of the past in our present circumstances. In the community, we are surrounded by the programs and institutions of past men and women who contributed and loved sacrificially. Such reflections pose a question: What are we doing with what we have inherited–to maintain, strengthen, and grow in our parish, personal life, and ministries, in our neighborhood and community? What do we wish to leave for others? To paraphrase a Scouts' slogan: How can we leave our campsite cleaner than we found it?

The Rev. Ronald L. Reed
St. James Episcopal Church
Wichita, Kansas

--- CY-16 ---

Thanksgiving Eve-Day

We at St. Thomas's do not have a Thanksgiving Day service. We find Thanksgiving morning is a difficult time for people to come and worship. Parishioners are traveling to Grandmother's. Family is coming for dinner and everyone is busy cooking. Church members are attending local high school football games. Instead, we worship on Thanksgiving Eve. Our twenty-four member men's chorus leads the worship, and we give each family a loaf of freshly baked bread. We fill tables in front of the altar full to overflowing with more than one hundred loaves of bread. The whole church smells like a bakery! We ask each family "to reserve" a loaf so that we are sure to have enough.

Tonight, as a symbol of God's love and care for us, we have these tables filled with bread. It smells just like a bakery here. Bread is a gift from God; in the *Lord's Prayer*, we ask: "Give us this day our daily bread." Tonight, [*St. Thomas's*] has a loaf of bread for every family. We have only one request. Please serve it as part of your Thanksgiving dinner. If you are visiting, take it with you. Tell everyone that it is a gift from the church in thanksgiving for all the ministers-members of our church.

The Bread of Life—The food that nourishes us and sustains us. Tonight, we will bless this bread as a sign of God's abundance and generosity. We can smell it—ummmm—see it, and after the service, you can come forward and feel it. We offer many kinds of bread, representing many nationalities and ethnic origins. We, as Christians, are called to give thanks for all generous gifts. Our offering is a very concrete way we say "Thank you" tonight to God. As pastor, I thank you for your generous spirit and your generous offerings.

—— SO-1 ——

Installation of Acolytes/Servers

In the Episcopal Church, we call the young men and women who assist the pastor acolytes and in the Roman Catholic Church, they are called servers. After they have completed their training, we publicly install our acolytes to the Guild of Acolytes. They are presented with a cross and a candle.

∽

This morning, we have installed three new acolytes into our Acolyte Guild. It is a wonderful way that they choose to practice their stewardship of time and abilities to serve Jesus Christ at his altar. I thank you for your practice of good stewardship that supports our Youth Ministry.

∽

Every Sunday at [*St. Thomas's*], our acolytes serve Jesus Christ at his altar. They are faithful stewards, who serve Christ by giving their time and abilities. This morning, [*insert names*] have been installed into our Guild. Our thanks to all of you who practice good stewardship by giving of your time, abilities, and money to support our children in this ministry.

—— SO-2 ——

Adult Education

Traditionally, adults in many Episcopal churches attended church while their children went to Sunday school. Following "graduation" from Sunday school, at about age twelve, education in the Scriptures and teachings of the church often stopped. Many adults today prefer this type of situation.

∽

Today, we gather to consider the stewardship of Scripture and our role as learners in the church. In practicing this aspect of our lives in service to God, we must exercise our willingness to "read, mark, and inwardly digest," the word of God. This form of stewardship involves active engagement with others in discussion of biblical passages so as to relate them to how we live our lives each day. Our informed contributions to the discussion are essential to doing God's will in the world.

> *Dr. Amelia J. Gearey*
> *Virginia Theological Seminary*

———— SO-3 ————

Air-Conditioning

In many parts of this country, the summers are hot—hot and humid. We have become accustomed to air conditioning and it is a must if one expects the congregation to come to church and listen on 100 degree plus days.

∽

This morning, outside, it is 101 degrees in the shade. But here inside, we are comfortable, thanks to our air-conditioning. We can worship without discomfort. I thank you for your offerings. Your gifts make it possible for us, as well as those who suffer health problems in the heat, to be here and join together to praise God. Thank you!

∽

It is hot and humid outside. I give thanks for all of you who have come to worship here today in the name of Jesus, in spite of the heat. I give thanks for our air-conditioning that enables me to preach and you to listen to the Word of God. Your faithful offerings, week by week, enable us to pay [*insert name of local utilities company*] in order that all who suffer from the heat can join us, regardless of the outside temperature, to share in our Christian community. Thank you!

⸺ SO-4 ⸺

Altar Guild

I recommend a public service of incorporation to the Altar Guild—those who care for this sacred place—in denominations in which this is appropriate. This service represents a personal stewardship of time and abilities and should be acknowledged.

∽

Setting: Installation of Altar Guild members

This morning, we installed [*insert names*] as members of our Altar Guild. They give of their time to care for our sacred and holy things. It is one way that they practice their stewardship of time and abilities. We are all called to give of ourselves to God through God's church and the world. Your generosity of time, abilities, and money enables [*St. Thomas's Church*] to have a beautiful and moving worship. Thank you.

∽

Setting: Communion Sunday morning.
(The altar looks especially beautiful)

Each Sunday, and on special days, we come to worship here at [*St. Thomas's*]. This act is the center of all we do. However, sometimes we take for granted the lovely flowers, the shining communion vessels, and the immaculate altar area. I want to thank the members of the Altar Guild who come to clean, polish, and care for our precious, holy things. My thanks to all of you. Thank you, too, for your generous donations to our Flower Fund. Because of your stewardship, we have a beautiful place in which to worship.

— SO-5 —

Annual Meeting

The annual meeting is held in every Episcopal Church. Every member of the congregation is invited. New vestry members and officers of the governing board are elected, financial reports are read, and the general health of the church is discussed. We at *St. Thomas's* make this a fun event. We precede the annual meeting with a roast beef dinner cooked by the members of the church and served by twenty-five of our own "singing waiters." They lead the congregation in singing a song about *St. Thomas's* with lots of humorous lines and laughter. When the actual meeting begins at 7:00 P.M., the congregation is well fed and mellow, with smiles on their faces.

Tonight, [*St. Thomas's Church*] will hold its annual meeting. This is the time when the officers and the members of the governing board report to you about their stewardship and the management and results of our personal stewardship of our time, abilities, and money during this past year. They will be sharing with you *good news*. This good news is the direct result of your personal stewardship and generosity. Thank you.

Tonight, [*St. Thomas's*] will hold its annual meeting. We will be electing members of the governing board to serve for the next [*insert number of years*]. I thank God for their practice of stewardship and for helping them to say "Yes" to leading the parish. Your giving of your time, ability, and money enables [*St. Thomas's*] to carry out its mission and vision.

—— SO-6 ——

Apportionment, Quota, and Assessment

Each Episcopal church is expected to make a pledge to support the diocese. Some dioceses assign the amount of the pledge, while in others, the amount is purely voluntary; however, it is a clear mandate that part of every dollar given to the individual local church goes to the diocese for missionary work.

∽

Today, in my stewardship minute, I want to talk about our giving to the Diocese of [insert name]. This year, we here at [insert name of church] are giving [insert amount] to further God's work and mission. Part of every dollar you give in your offering goes to reach out and change the world in the name of Christ. I thank you for your generosity. When you read in your diocesan newspaper about all the good things being done in our diocese, remember–you helped make them happen.

∽

As part of our church's stewardship of time, ability, and money,we here at [insert name of church] pledge our full apportionment to the Diocese of [insert name]. This year we are contributing [insert amount], because God has blessed us and we want to share our abundance with the diocese. Remember, from every dollar you give and every dollar we receive for our budget, a share goes beyond these walls to change the world! On behalf of our bishop, I want to thank you for your generosity.

— SO-7 —

Baptism

I believe that baptism should normally be done as part of regular worship or special Feast Days. That is the context for these services.

∞

Setting: Baptism Sunday

Today, we witnessed the baptism of [*insert names*] and we welcome them into our Christian community. We promise to do all that we can to support them in their new life in Christ. We do this through our weekly offering of our time, abilities, and money. Some will teach them, but the money we all give will enable [*St. Thomas's*] to support [*insert names*] in their Christian life through fine church school materials, clean classrooms, and a welcoming Christian community. Thank you for your faithful stewardship.

∞

Today, we all took part in an adoptive service. Through their baptism, we adopted these children into [*St. Thomas's Church*]. We vowed to care for these children as members of our church family. Your generous gifts of time, abilities, and money enable us to do that. We are a welcoming Christian community that finds its identity in the name of Jesus Christ. Thank you for your generosity.

— SO-8 —

Blood Drive

Once a year, we have a blood drive in our church. This donation entitles everyone in the congregation to share in the Red Cross Blood Bank.

∞

Some might say that we have taken stewardship to a *new low*. We have always talked about your giving your time, your ability, and your money to the church, but now, we want your *blood*! There is no way to make any kind of artificial blood. It cannot be purchased anywhere; it can only be given. We pray that you who are able to do so will come next [*insert day*] between the hours of [*insert time*], and give the Blood of Life.

∞

Yesterday, [*insert number*] members of our church gathered in an act of stewardship–our Blood Drive. The money from our offering this morning is as vital to the church as that blood was for our community. It brings health to a world in need of God's love and reconciliation. I thank all who gave blood yesterday, and all who have given generously of their money this morning.

─── SO-9 ───

Children and Worship

Young children are often absent from worship. They are either placed in the nursery or in a Sunday school class so they will not disturb the adults at prayer. This comment discusses the importance of the responsibility of all Christians for teaching our children to worship.

∞

Today let us consider the gift of teaching another about God. We are called to share the message of the gospel, yet many of us are not called to be evangelists. There is one very significant way that we can teach another person about God. Share your love of God with a young child. Teach children the love of God by welcoming them into your presence, even in church. Teach them how to worship by allowing them to watch and imitate you in prayer.

Dr. Amelia J. Gearey
Virginia Theological Seminary

—— SO-10 ——

Church School Opening
September

We begin our Church School dedication with a simple liturgy for the dedication of the teachers, children, and parents, to acknowledge their stewardship.

☙

Setting: Opening of Church School and Induction of Teachers

This morning we took part in the dedication of our Church School teachers. They are giving of themselves, their stewardship of time and ability, to teach our children. Through your generous weekly offerings, we have the best church school materials available, clean, warm classrooms, and a giving, caring Christian community. With your offerings, we are caring for our children. I thank God for your faithful stewardship.

☙

Each Sunday, we have [*insert number*] children and [*insert number*] teachers gather for our Church School classes. We are indeed fortunate that many of our parents take their baptismal promises seriously "for seeing that their child is brought up in the Christian faith and life." Here at [*St. Thomas's*], our children are not our future, but our *present*. They bring life and God's love to us. Thank you for your generous offerings that enable us to share this "love of Jesus" with our children.

—— SO-11 ——

Choir Sunday–Blessing

On the last Sunday in June that the choir sings, we have the members come to the altar for a Blessing of Thanksgiving, in appreciation for their leadership in praising the Lord.

☙

At the end of the service this morning, we will ask our choir to come to the altar for a Blessing, to thank them for their stewardship of their time and abilities in leading us in worship every Sunday. We appreciate their faithfulness and dedication. I also want to thank you for your faithful and generous gifts of money each week. Because of you, our choir has new music, good robes, a quality organ, and a fine director of Music Ministries.

Each Sunday, our choir leads us in praising God in joy for all creation. We appreciate the faithful stewardship of those who give their time at rehearsals and on Sundays, and the use of their abilities in singing and in playing instruments for the glory of God. We appreciate our music director, who takes responsibility for leading and supporting all those who are involved in our music ministry. We thank all who give of their time and talent. Today we will bless our choir. I want to thank you all for your generous giving. Because of you, we have a wonderful expression of your love and praise to God.

—— SO-12 ——

Church School Graduation and Closing

On the second Sunday in June, we have a special service at which our children each make a class presentation and receive a pin—the Holy Spirit, a Cross, or another symbol—for participating in our church school program. It is a gift of their stewardship of time and ability.

We applaud our children for their wonderful presentations this morning. They have practiced their stewardship of time and abilities. We thank their teachers for their faithful stewardship, and we thank you for yours. By your offerings, our children have had the finest materials, clean and warm classrooms, and loving support in their learning. We all should feel good this morning, as we celebrate and give thanks for our children.

∽

We give thanks for our children. Here at [*St. Thomas's,*] we do not see them as our future, but as our present. They bring us life and joy. We thank their parents for sharing their children with us this past year. I thank you for your faithful stewardship. Your weekly offerings have provided our children with an excellent Church School program–the results of which we have experienced here this morning.

———— SO-13 ————

Confirmation/Reception

In the Episcopal and Roman Catholic Churches, Confirmation is administered only by the bishop. Normally, there are classes for young adults, and hands are laid on the candidate for God's grace. The same premise would apply for all denominations that practice a service of Confirmation.

Usually, the loose offering conducted at this time goes to the Bishop's Discretionary Fund.

∽

Today, we welcome Bishop, [*insert name*] who has just confirmed and received [*insert number*] of young people and adults. In practicing their stewardship, our young people have been studying, doing service projects, and preparing for this day for the past year. Your generous support of their ministry has demonstrated good stewardship. Our loose offering today will support the ministry of our bishop through his Discretionary Fund.

∽

Today, it is a joy to welcome Bishop [*insert name*]to [*St. Thomas's Church*]. The name of our denomination, Episcopal, comes from the Greek word for bishop–*episcopos*. We are a church led by bishops. Our offering this morning will go to the Bishop's Discretionary Fund. Our giving is our way of supporting our bishop as he goes to minister to our diocese in the name of Jesus.

⏤ SO-14 ⏤

Confirmation–Youth

We have a year-long preparation for seventh-and eighth-grade youth who will be confirmed by the bishop. The entire parish supports their effort with time, abilities, and money. Part of this preparation is the teaching of stewardship.

∞

Next Sunday, following a year of preparation, our Youth Confirmation Class will be confirmed by Bishop [*insert name*]. I want to thank their teacher and all of you who, through your faithful stewardship of time, abilities, and money, have supported these young people. These fine young boys and girls are a credit to our church. Thank you for your support.

∞

Today I want to thank the members of our Youth Confirmation Class for their stewardship of their time, abilities, and money here at [*St. Thomas's Church*]. They have worked hard to prepare for confirmation, giving of themselves and preparing to take on adult responsibilities within our church. We admire their dedication and commitment. I also want to thank you, the congregation, for your generous support. Your faithful stewardship, week by week, makes this day possible.

⟶ SO-15 ⟵

Cursillo Weekend

Cursillo is a Spanish word meaning "short course." It signifies an ecumenical renewal program which is a short course in Christianity. It is a lay-led movement for mission, whose centerpiece is a three-day weekend, normally beginning on a Thursday evening and ending late Sunday afternoon. Those who are attending their first weekend are called candidates; those who lead the weekend are called staff.

∞

Today, [*insert number*] members of our congregation are attending a Cursillo weekend. We will pray for them when we receive your offering. They are giving of their time and abilities to experience a weekend of living in a Christian community. We give thanks to those who are sponsoring these candidates, giving of their time, money, and abilities.

∞

This morning our parish is sponsoring [*insert number*] members of our congregation, who are attending a *Cursillo* weekend. A *Cursillo* is a short course on Christianity. Our thanks to those who have supported these candidates through their stewardship of time, ability, and money. Our entire parish continually strives to become a strong, caring Christian community. Your generous offerings enable us to be such a community.

⟶ SO-16 ⟵

Diocesan Convention–Sunday Before

The diocese is our corporate way of organizing our life in the Episcopal Church. Dioceses are regions normally representative of a state or section of a state.

∞

On [*insert day*], the clergy and lay delegates of our diocese will meet at [*insert location*] to make decisions affecting our life together. For the delegates from our parish, we are exercising our stewardship, giving of our time, ability, and money. We need you to practice your stewardship this week through prayer, asking for God's discernment to be within us and affirming that our life in Jesus Christ is an abundant one.

∞

Our Diocesan Convention is the coming together of both clergy and lay delegates from every church to worship and listen to God's voice. It is the way we gather to practice our common stewardship of time, ability, and money. I thank you for your generous offerings. Your faithful financial support of the Diocese of [*insert name*] enables us to do the work proclaiming the lordship of Jesus Christ by word and deed.

—— SO-17 ——

Disaster–Natural

I suggest each parish keep a box of Presiding Bishop's Fund envelopes in the office. In that way, following a natural disaster, on the very next Sunday, a collection can be taken for immediate relief. We insert one of these envelopes in the Sunday bulletin and continue to include them for the entire month, thus giving the congregation an opportunity to help. We also have a collection of plain white envelopes and a label stamp maker so that we may take a special collection for anyone in need.

∞

Setting: Sunday after a natural disaster
(such as when the floods hit the Midwest)

This past week, we have seen the devastation brought on by [*insert disaster*]. I always thank you for your generous offerings to St. Thomas's, but this week I ask you to make a special gift to the Presiding Bishop's Fund with the envelope found in your bulletin. Our Presiding Bishop's Fund is there in our name providing for the disaster victims. Since the time of Saint Paul, Christians have taken collections and sent them to those in need. Please be generous.

∞

Setting: Sunday following a Major Disaster
(such as the Rwandan Civil War)

This past week, we have been deeply touched by the tragedy that is taking place in [*insert region*]. This morning we are taking a collection to [*insert specific purpose*]. It is amazing to me that by the simple act of writing a check, my wife and I can help save a life!

—— SO-18 ——

Church Burnings

In the summer of 1996, many denominations and churches responded to the burning of the Black churches in the South. These are two examples of how we addressed this problem with a special offering.

∞

Today, as you open your bulletin, you will find a special envelope to help rebuild the Black churches that have been burned throughout the South. We are now being given an opportunity to vote for justice and condemn this evil by making a generous offering of our prayers and money. I thank you for your generous weekly offerings, and I know, today, you will give to make a difference in our nation.

∞

This Sunday we have a special way to thank God for all the gifts God has so generously given to us and to stand with other Christians to rebuke those who have been burning Black churches. Evil is with us and can be overcome only by God and godly people fighting for good. I thank you for your generosity in the past and give thanks for all of those who have made gifts and are making gifts for these people, to say we are one in Christ.

—— SO-19 ——

Ecumenical

A growing number of local churches these days are committed to grassroots ecumenical cooperation through area ministerial associations and other groups. Through our stewardship, we support these cooperative ministries.

∞

This past Monday, our governing board approved a grant from our church to [*insert the name and description of the specific group being assisted*]. Together with other local churches, we work there to proclaim the gospel by word and deed. I want to thank you for your faithful stewardship that enables us to serve those most needing our help. Your gifts of money each week really do make a difference in the world.

∞

You know some of the good work that is made possible by your stewardship of time, ability, and money to [*St. Thomas's*]. However, many of you may be unaware of how we practice stewardship in working with the other churches in our area. We gather together through [*insert own local church groups*]. We are doing our mission by serving those in need in the spirit of cooperation, rather than acting in competition with the other churches. Thank you for your faithful stewardship that makes this possible.

---— SO-20 —---

Evening Prayer

"I will bless the Lord who gives me counsel; in the night also my heart instructs me. I keep the Lord always before me; because he is my right hand, I shall not be moved."
Psalm 16:7-8

If we look out from this place, we know that the light of day is soon gone. We reflect on what has come to pass today. We anticipate an increase of darkness and quieting of our lives. In rest, we make our evening prayers thanking God for what has been today and asking for a good and holy night. As we rest in the peace of divine oversight of our night, may we count our blessings, remember opportunities for extending God's love well engaged. Yet also, we can with divine grace look forward to the dawning of a new day. May we recommit ourselves for tomorrow to new challenges and to face those things left unattended today that we may accomplish tomorrow. May the stewardship of our lives be accomplished for the sake of the good news of our Lord. End the day well and in thanksgiving.

The Rev. Ronald Reed
St. James Episcopal Church
Wichita, Kansas

⟶ SO-21 ⟶

First Communion

We at *St. Thomas's* have special communion preparation in which parents meet with lay members and clergy for six weeks of classes in order that these parents may teach their children as a family unit, using Gretchen Pritchard's book, *Alleluia, Amen.* The children prepare a workbook and a scrapbook of their learning experiences, which they present at the offering. This is an example of our own special service. It could be amended to fit each individual parish.

∞

This morning, [*insert number*] of our children will be receiving Holy Communion. As their stewardship, they will be placing their communion books in the offering plates. These books represent six weeks of their time and abilities. The books will be placed on the altar and blessed and will be available for the congregation, as their extended family, to read at Hospitality Hour. As part of my stewardship, I will read them and write a personal response for each child. I thank you all for your generous giving that makes all of this possible.

∞

For the past six weeks, our parents have been meeting for holy communion classes so that they would be able to instruct their children about holy communion. I thank them for their stewardship of time and ability. They recognize that quantity time is no substitute for quality time, and they give generously of that. Our children will give their communion books as their offering today. I want to thank the entire congregation for loving, accepting, and encouraging our children. The children know that they are loved here. Thank you for your generosity of spirit and money.

SO-22

Food Collection

We belong to an ecumenical agency that acts in our name for Christian charity. Our local group, called Assistance Center of Towson Churches, has a membership of forty churches. Each church takes a month during the year to provide for the food closet. We normally begin our month of supplying the food closet on Super Bowl Sunday, which we have renamed Supper Bowl Sunday.

Today is "Supper Bowl Sunday" at [*St. Thomas's*]. As part of your stewardship, you have all been asked to bring in a bag of food to feed the hungry. Because of this stewardship, the hungry will eat during February. We give thanks for our Youth Confirmation Class, who, as part of their stewardship, will collect this food and deliver it to the [*A.C.T.C.*].

Today, we are collecting food for the hungry. This is one way we practice our stewardship mission to feed the hungry and bring compassion to the world. Remember—no gift is too large; the food and money you give will bring life and health to our community.

—— SO-23 ——

Food Pantry–Emergency

With the support of our Council on Ministries and the blessing of our Administrative Board, our Emergency Food Pantry is open on the last Thursday of every month from 6:00 to 7:30 in the evening. Our pantry is the only one of its kind in Baltimore County open in the evening and available to the working poor. Approximately twenty-six families take advantage of our hospitality each month. Everyone who comes to us for food is required to have a home with a kitchen in order to prepare the food that we give them. The food comes from food drives held in local schools and from you, our congregation, contributing to the Sharing Basket found in the main lobby of our church.

The Emergency Food Pantry is more than food. Recipients tell us that this is the only place where they come for help and everyone is always smiling. It takes the time and talents of eight to twelve volunteers to run the pantry each month. Thank you for your contributions of food, your prayers, and your money that keep our building warm and the doors open. "And the king will answer them, 'Truly. I say to you, as you did it to one of the least of these, my brethren, you did it to me'" (Matthew 25:40, *RSV*).

> *Catherine A. Ritter*
> *Towson United Methodist Church*
> *Towson, Maryland*

—— SO-24 ——

Funeral–Following Sunday

I believe Christians should be buried from the church. Today, since many of our parishioners are choosing direct cremation, a memorial service is held at the church.

∽

On Thursday, we buried Jane, a long-time faithful member of our congregation. Jane loved our Lord, and we trust that, with God's mercy, she now dwells with God in Paradise. Because of your faithful stewardship, we gave thanks for her life with a Christian burial. Your generous weekly offerings help us to have a warm and beautiful church in which her family and friends can come together.

∞

On Thursday evening, our congregation gathered to give thanks for the life of Charles. Charles loved the parish. He practiced exceptional stewardship in giving his time, using his abilities, and generously sharing his resources with *St. Thomas's* Church. We will miss him. Our condolences go out to his family. His giving of himself strengthened our church.

— SO-25 —

Healing–Prayers

At every service of worship at St. Thomas's, we offer prayers of healing. Normally, we give specific names; we also mention those known only in the hearts of the worshippers.

∞

Part of our stewardship is taking time, developing our ability to pray–to communicate with God in Prayers of Intercession for those in need of God's healing. In practicing good Christian stewardship, it is not time or abilities, or money, but all three, given to make known God's love for this world. We are healed not to retire from God's service, but to serve God's world. We are always called upon to practice good stewardship.

∞

Sometimes, in a conversation at school or work or at home, we are told, "I have cancer. I am going to have open-heart surgery. I am going through a divorce after many years of marriage." Many times, the response is: "I am sorry to hear that. Well, good luck!" For Christians, I believe that it is not luck, but prayers that make the difference. Next time, say, "I will keep you in my prayers." Do this as part of your stewardship. Pray for the person every day and at church on Sunday. It is a wonderful way to build a deep friendship with that person and with God.

—— SO-26 ——

Healing Service

Every Wednesday at 10:00 A.M., we have a service of Holy Eucharist and Laying on of Hands for healing.

∞

This past week, I had the privilege of laying hands of healing, in the name of Jesus, on several of our parishioners. We here at [*St. Thomas's*] believe in God's power through Jesus Christ to heal body, mind, spirit, and soul. This is part of our stewardship of our gifts from the Lord. You are each present at this service. We remember the sick members of this parish and all of this congregation because, through your faithful stewardship, you are all a part of everything that this church does.

∞

Do you believe in God's healing power? We do as a congregation here at [*St. Thomas's Church*]. Each time we celebrate the Eucharist, we proclaim by word and deeds the healing power of Jesus Christ. Whether you come on a weekday or Sunday, we *expect* Jesus Christ to heal, to bring his peace and comfort to those in need in body, mind, spirit, and soul. By your faithful stewardship, we stand here as a hospital for sinners rather than a country club for saints.

━━ SO-27 ━━

Heritage Fund–Planned Giving

The Heritage Fund is a perpetual fund, the income from which is to be used for repairs and major improvements to the church building and grounds. It is similar to the Endowment Fund in many churches.

∞

Today, as part of [*St. Thomas's*] stewardship, I want to share with you an explanation of the Heritage Fund. This fund now has [*insert amount*] in assets. The income is used for the care of the actual church building and the surrounding property. We encourage our church members to remember [*St. Thomas's*] in their wills–it is a way your gifts can care for our church buildings so that they will be here to minister to future generations.

∞

Here at [*St. Thomas's Church*], we give of our time, abilities, and money in many ways. Today, I want to thank all of those who have gone before us in this church. The Heritage Fund exists to care for capital funds and major improvements. Gifts are received through bequests and in memory of loved ones. They enable our buildings and grounds to be a fitting place for worship and ministry. I thank all who have remembered the Heritage Fund in their wills.

SO-28

Homebound Communions

I suggest that the name "shut-ins" be abolished and replaced with the word "homebound," which is more positive and descriptive. Monthly, my associates and I bring communion to our homebound members. In many churches, lay eucharistic ministers bring communion weekly or monthly to the home. This practice is fine, but, in my opinion, it does not replace a call from the pastor, since these are the members who cannot get to church to hear the preacher's sermons.

Each Sunday, when we gather to celebrate communion together, we set aside a part of the bread and wine and save it in the aumbry in the chancel. Each week, Pastor [*insert name*] and I take that bread and wine, consecrated here in church, to the homebound. We share a simple communion service and you are there with us. Thank you for your generous stewardship. Your offerings, given faithfully, enable Pastor [*insert name*] and me to be there in the houses, apartments, and nursing homes.

Each week, the clergy of [*St. Thomas's*] go out to the nursing homes and homes of our congregation and bring communion to our homebound members. At our church, we do not cast aside those faithful members who have left us a fine legacy of caring. Your faithful stewardship of your time and your ability, as well as your offerings of money, enable the clergy to be present with them. As part of *their* stewardship, our eucharistic ministers assist in this caring. My thanks to you all.

— SO-29 —

Hospital Calls

Calling on the sick, especially those in the hospital, is a top priority among all clergy I know. We believe that when we enter a hospital room, we bring the parish with us, for we go connected by prayer and it is through the members' generosity that we have the time to be there. All clergy have had the experience of representing almost a godly presence to those troubled souls.

This past week, I spent an afternoon at [*insert name*] Hospital with the family of one of our church members, waiting for him to come out of surgery. I am happy to report that he is doing well and hopes to be home again soon. As I waited and prayed with the family, I thought about you and your stewardship. Your prayers sustained [*insert name*] and your generous offerings of time, ability, and money enabled me to be there. Remember, when you hear that Pastor [*insert name*] was at the hospital—smile, feel good—for you were with me!

On Wednesday, I drove to [*insert name*] Hospital to make a call on a member of our parish. It is a huge, confusing place; it can be overwhelming. When I arrived at the parishioner's room, she smiled, tears welled up—I was a familiar face in the confusion and fear. While I shared communion, I thought of you last Sunday—how you came, prayed, praised, and gave your offerings—and because of you, I could be there in that hospital room celebrating communion, sharing Jesus and you. Thank you. You are a special gift from God!

SO-30

Hospitality Hour

We no longer have a "Coffee Hour" at St. Thomas's, for two reasons. First, we not only serve coffee, but also tea, punch, juice, and doughnut holes. Second, and most important, we are serving Christian hospitality to all who come to worship at our Sunday service.

Each Sunday, following our service, everyone is invited to come to Hospitality Hour. Hospitality Hour is paid for by your generous stewardship. Your offerings make it possible. When you come and see a Sunday guest with a cup of tea, engaging in a lively conversation with one of our regular members, you are seeing the results of your stewardship. When you see children of all ages with their doughnut holes and smiles on their faces from ear to ear, that is your stewardship. Thank you for your generosity that makes [St. Thomas's] a growing, welcoming church.

Hospitality is an ancient Hebrew and Christian concept–to welcome the stranger. The Letter to the Hebrews tells us we entertain angels unbeknownst to us when we offer hospitality. Thanks to your giving of time, ability, and money, [St. Thomas] is an hospitable church. We know that God wants us to reach out and welcome the newcomer. Thank you, for by your offering of yourselves, we are welcoming those whom God has brought to our church!

——— SO-31 ———

Incorporation of New Members

I believe that every congregation needs to develop an incorporation service for newcomers—a liturgical way beyond confirmation to welcome individuals and families into the parish family.

Today, we welcomed and incorporated [*insert number*] new households into [*St. Thomas's Church*]. It is wonderful to have you all as part of our worshiping community and church family. We accept you as fellow stewards of our congregation. Together, we strive to practice good stewardship—management of our time, ability, and money to build up the community of Jesus Christ.

It is wonderful to welcome our newest members to [*St. Thomas's Church*] this morning. Our special thanks to our greeters who stand with me, at the back of the church, and to the welcoming committee who, as part of their stewardship of time, talents, and money, work to make our guests feel welcome. Your stewardship of time, ability, and money has made a difference. We are giving thanks to you.

—— SO-32 ——

Labor Day

Setting: The Sunday of the last weekend of summer, when we remember and lift up the value of work.

Today, Labor Day has come to represent the last three-day weekend of vacation, the end of summer, and the beginning of the school year. Originally, Labor Day was a day set aside to appreciate those whose hard physical labor made our nation strong. It was seen as a day of stewardship and an acknowledgment of the value of the use of our time, ability, and money. Our weekly offering comes from our labor. It is our way of acknowledging God, who gave us our stewardship over His creation.

Labor Day used to be a day of great parades in all the cities, as union members walked proudly before their families. Labor was seen as good—work that gave us the material necessities and comforts. But work is actually so much more than that. It embodies our share of creating in the world in which God has given us so much responsibility. We are all workers in God's kingdom. There is no retirement from discipleship. Our stewardship is how we manage all that God has given us. Your offering today of time, ability, and money is our human way of saying "Thank you!"

---— SO-33 —---

Legacies I

The Bustle in a House
The Morning after Death
Is solemnest of industries
Enacted upon Earth.

The Sweeping up the Heart
And putting Love away
We shall not want to use again
Until Eternity.

Emily Dickinson

∽

The bustle in the house the morning after death. The sweeping up of the heart. If I died tomorrow, or if you died, what would we be remembered for? What kind of responses would our lives bring to mind? What kind of legacy do we want to leave behind? Is it money or property? Attitudes or beliefs? Changed lives? What do we want to be remembered for?

I knew a woman who lived a very modest life and died a very wealthy woman. She wanted to leave everything she had to her college and to her church. And for this, she will be remembered. All those years, she was terribly worried that her money wouldn't last, and that all her life savings would be spent on nursing care. She was terribly upset. But in her last few days, a peace came over her and she seemed to shed her anxiety and fear. It was as if I watched her let go and move from this world to a place where she was free, where she didn't need to worry because God was in control, not she. I prayed for her and gave thanks to God for her legacy, but I wished that she had been able to trust God earlier and know the peace of God long before her death. I pray that each of us might know the peace that comes from faith in God long before–years before–the hour of our death.

The Rev. Phebe L. Coe
Church of the Epiphany
Odenton, Maryland

—— SO-34 ——

Legacies II

How to keep–is there any any, is there none such, nowhere
known some, bow or brooch or braid or brace, lace, latch or
catch or key to keep
Back beauty, keep it, beauty, beauty, beauty, from vanishing
away?
...Give beauty back, beauty, beauty, beauty, back to God, beauty's
self and beauty's giver.

Gerald Manley Hopkins

∞

What is it that we treasure so much that we are afraid to use it?
Afraid to take it out of hiding and enjoy it, share it, use it? What
kind of treasures and resources have you been given? What are
you doing with them? What kind of legacy do you want to leave
behind? Is it money or property? Attitudes or beliefs? Changed
lives? What do *you* want to leave behind?

A few years ago my house was robbed. Among the items
taken was a large gray flannel bag full of family jewelry that I had
tucked away for safekeeping. Occasionally, I would take it out
and examine its contents–trying on this, admiring that. It was
only after the bag and all its contents were gone that I realized
what I might have been able to do with those things. Actually, I
could have kept them and always enjoyed them–if I had given
them away! These inanimate objects could have been sold and
transformed–silver and gold melted by God's love into instruments to help change lives. I wish I had done this. It is too late
for that particular bag of treasure, but it is not too late for us. May
we be able to give our treasures to God and God's purposes, for
really safekeeping!

The Rev. Phebe L. Coe
The Church of the Epiphany
Odenton, Maryland

--- SO-35 ---

Lutheran World Relief

Lutheran World Relief may well be the world's most effective agency dealing with world hunger.

In Angola, at one of the refugee camps that suddenly sprang up in just a couple of weeks as people fled the chaos of the Hutu-Tutsi wars, Lutheran World Hunger had been providing water, food, and clothing.

When word spread through the camp that some executives of the organization were coming to the camp, the people came out of their plastic tents, waving colorful quilts that Lutheran women in the United States had sewn for them. They waved the quilts like flags, and cheered and cheered and cheered their thanks as the Lutherans walked down the center of the "main street" of that refugee city. That is what our few dollars for world hunger means in just one tiny place in this world.

Bishop George Paul Mocko
Evangelical Lutheran Church in America
Delaware-Maryland Synod

--- SO-36 ---

Morning Prayer

"But the hour is coming and is now here, when the true worshippers will worship the Father in spirit and truth, for the Father seeks such as these to worship Him."
John 4:23

∞

The new day is celebrated in our morning prayers together. Another day is added to our lives for our enjoyment and use. We have begun this day well, because we have gathered to worship God and remember our relationship with our Lord. We are celebrating and cherishing this new day. It is a gift to us. And how shall we go forth from this house of worship this day? We are called by Christ and his church to carry the message of good news into our daily lives. How will our stewardship of this day unfold? Into what relationship, task, or fun will we carry this wonderful news? How can we take this daily gift of life and find a gentle application of Christ's love to build on the good news?

The Rev. Ronald L. Reed
St. James Episcopal Church
Wichita, Kansas

——— SO-37 ———

Music

"Stained Glass Bluegrass Sunday" is an annual event when our choir teams up with a local Bluegrass Band to lead the congregation in the worship of God through the singing of many of the old (but rarely sung) songs that had their roots in nineteenth century revivalism and twentieth century rural piety.

Today, we take literally the psalmist's encouragement to "make a joyful noise to the Lord. Break forth into joyous song and sing praises." Music and singing have always been among the ways that God's people have praised God and given expression to the joyful experience of God's grace in their lives. Even stodgy old John Calvin, our spiritual ancestor, was moved on at least one occasion to write a hymn.

Another way we give thanks to God is through our gifts and offerings. They not only make possible the ministry of music that enhances our worship Sunday after Sunday, but they also bring joy and hope to the lives of others through our local and denominational outreach ministries.

Therefore, with great joy and thanksgiving to God for all God's blessings, including the blessing of music, let us continue our worship through the giving and receiving of the morning offering.

The Rev. Mary Doyle Morgan
Maryland Presbyterian Church USA

—— SO-38 ——

New Congregation Committee

As pastor of St. Thomas's, I am involved as a member of the New Congregation Committee. We need to thank our congregation because as part of their stewardship, they provide the pastor with time and use of his abilities for God's work beyond the local church to the diocese and the national church. The New Congregation Committee is responsible for founding new congregations in the Episcopal Diocese of Maryland.

⬠

Jesus Christ tells us that we are to go out to the ends of the earth to preach the gospel. In today's world, that might very well be in our neighboring towns and counties. I believe we were not created for the church, but that the church was created for the people that we might know Jesus Christ as our Lord and Savior.

⬠

All of our time, ability, and money are gifts which God has given to us. I thank God for your stewardship of money that allows me to serve on the New Congregation Committee and to use my time and abilities to help found new congregations that will proclaim the name of Jesus. My time is your gift to the [*insert the name of your church governing body*]. Your money enables the mission of Jesus Christ to take place through the area. Thank you for your faithful offerings.

─── SO-39 ───

Novitiation–Bar Mitzvah

In the Episcopal Church, this ceremony is like a group Bar Mitzvah. The Saturday evening before the bishop comes for Confirmation, the entire Youth Confirmation Class prepares and conducts the whole service of worship. Each candidate invites his or her parents, godparents, and friends with printed invitations.

☙

This is a wonderful evening for our Youth Confirmation Class. We are proud of you! Thank you for leading us in worship, preaching the sermons, and praising God. Our thanks also to your parents, whose stewardship of their time, talents, and money have brought you to [St. Thomas's] week by week. Sometimes church members may wonder: "Does my offering really make a difference?" Look around you at our Confirmation Class this evening–Is there any doubt? Thank you!

☙

Tomorrow, Bishop [insert name] comes for confirmation. He will confirm the [insert number] young people who are leading our worship tonight. They are well prepared for this ceremony. Our thanks go to you for your faithful stewardship of time. Your children are here because you brought them. You have supported them by your example, your discipline, and your love. Our special thanks to their teacher, [insert name]. And our thanks, too, for your giving of money, for with your financial support, we have been able to act out of abundance.

—— SO-40 ——

Nursing Homes–Services

One of the ways we serve the community is by conducting services at nursing homes. We receive no compensation for these services. This ministry is very important, but it is seldom held up as part of the stewardship of our members to help care for the world.

☙

This past week, I thought of you all as I was leading worship at [*insert name of nursing home*], where each month in the church calendar, I visit and bring the sacrament we have shared and consecrated on Sunday to be shared ecumenically with the men and women there. I preach and lay hands of healing on each one of them. I am able to be there because of your stewardship. The money you give each Sunday enables me to have the time to use my God-given abilities to preach and bring the love of Jesus Christ to those in special need of this love. Thank you for sending me. Your faithful stewardship makes it possible.

☙

We all are aging every day, and some of us will spend our last days in a nursing home. Because we here at [*St. Thomas's*] want to reach out to those in nursing homes, we visit, hold services, and bring communion to both our local church members and nonmembers alike. This reaching out to help change our world is part of our vision, supported by your faithful stewardship. Your personal stewardship and our vision to "worship and serve in Jesus' name," enable me to be sent there. Thank you for your generous offerings and the gifts that make all of this possible.

—— SO-41 ——

Planned Giving I
Outreach Fund

The Outreach Fund, begun by our previous rector, is a model fund for those who do not want a general endowment to hurt good stewardship The income from this fund can be used only to help parishioners in need and for ministry outside the parish church.

Today, I want to share with you one of the ways [*St. Thomas's Church*] practices good stewardship–the Outreach Fund. This fund exists to help church members in financial need and the church's ministry beyond our own congregation. If you or one of our church members is in financial need, please speak to me. It will be held in strictest confidence. Our thanks to all who have made gifts and bequests to the Outreach Fund and to those who have mentioned it in their wills.

This past week, our finance chairman sent checks to various local ministries and community projects [*insert name of groups*]. This giving is part of our church's ministry to change the world. My deepest thanks to all who have made gifts to this fund and to those who have remembered the [*St. Thomas's Church*] Outreach Fund in their wills. Also, I thank you for your faithful Sunday offerings, for with these, too, we can work to change the world.

—— SO-42 ——

Planned Giving II
How Will They Remember Me?

It is likely that many of us have probably been through the exercise of writing our own epitaphs. We see the announcement in the newspapers about someone we know who has died. Or we read what is said about a family member or an elderly person who has passed away, and we wonder what "they" would say about us.

What will they say about me? How will they remember me?

What is perhaps more important while I am still alive is for me to think about *how I want them to remember me*. How I *will* be remembered may, in fact, be a different question from how I *want* to be remembered!

Do I have time enough left in my life to do the things I should do and be the person I want them to remember me to have been?

Today is the first day of the rest of my life. What will it be from now on?

Fred Osborn
Episcopal Church Foundation

—— SO-43 ——

Planned Giving III
What I Wish For My Children

I was privileged to be asked by the headmaster of my daughter's school to give a speech at the baccalaureate service before her graduation a few years ago. In preparing for the speech, I found myself thinking rather profoundly *about what I wished for my daughter.* I thought of things like happiness, fulfilling relationships, an exciting job, that she have the chance to make a contribution to society, that she be a nice person and have a lot of friends.

And then I hit on what I really wanted for her—I want her to be *generous*—for her *own* sake. I want her to feel the love that God and her family have for her. I want her to be able to confront the fear of not having enough (a fear that our culture is doing its damnedest to exploit!) and recognize that by *giving,* she will find deeper relationships and more lasting values. By becoming involved in organizations and causes bigger than she is, she will be on her way to finding herself in this huge, complicated world.

What do you wish for *your* children? What would you say in a baccalaureate speech at their graduation?

Fred Osborn
Episcopal Church Foundation

—— SO-44 ——

Planned Giving IV
How Much Is Enough?

Our culture is filled with phrases that convince us that "just a little more" would be "enough." Indeed, the market economy under which our capitalist system thrives *must* establish a sense of scarcity in order to survive.

It has been said that the modern American dream is to use money you don't have; to buy things you don't need; to impress people you don't even know.

Since we are bombarded with that message of scarcity day in and day out, can the church be the one place where, for a measly one hour a week, we talk about the abundance God has given us?

Can it be the place where we celebrate that God has given us "enough"? Isn't that what the gospel message is all about? "I am come that you may have life, and have it more abundantly."

That abundant life is here and now, revealed in how we look at what we have(recognizing our lives are as filled with gifts from God and from others); celebrating what we have, instead of complaining about what we do not have.

Generosity comes from the heart that is overflowing with a sense of abundance It is to the generous that Christ promises the abundant life.

Fred Osborn
Episcopal Church Foundation

—— SO-45 ——

Planned Giving V
Too Little Too Late

A very nice man came to me some time ago and said that he was worried about the continuation of his support to the church after he died. I suggested that he make a provision in his will for the church that would provide an income about equal to his pledge.

A year later, he came to me with the same concern. I asked him if he was happy with the way his will was written and he remembered that he had wanted to add the provision that we had talked about, but that he had not done so as yet.

A few months later, our church started its Legacy Club for members who have remembered the church in their estate plans. I approached him to see if he would be willing to put his name and picture on a letter to parishioners and talk about the Legacy Club and what it meant to him. He said he was terribly embarrassed—he had fully intended to change his will to include the church, but he just hadn't gotten around to it yet. He would get right on to it!

That fall, he was diagnosed with terminal cancer. I did not have the heart to ask him if he had "gotten around to it yet." Nor did I have the courage to ask him if he were comfortable with the provisions his will included. He died that winter.

It turned out that he had never gotten around to it. The tragedy was not that the church did not receive the money—we will receive other funds from other sources. The tragedy is that this good man, whose heart was in the right place, just didn't get to do what he really wanted to do in continuing his support for an organization that he really admired and wanted to help.

Fred Osborn
Episcopal Church Foundation

—— SO-46 ——

Planned Giving VI
Managing Our Blessings

Those of us who recognize the blessings God has bestowed on us are often quite aware of our responsibility to nurture, care for, and "steward" those blessings.

But what are we doing about the use of those blessings after we no longer need them?

We recognize our responsibility to be stewards of our resources while we live. But what about being a steward of those resources after we die? If we are able, should we leave resources to continue caring for the things we cared for while we were alive?

Of course, first, we should make prudent provision for the well-being of our families. The Prayer Book directs the minister of the congregation to instruct the people about that.

It also instructs people to make provisions, if they are able, to provide bequests for charitable and religious uses.

Have you made plans to manage your blessings after you are not around to manage them for yourself? Writing a will is not a difficult process. Getting to it seems to be!

You will feel much better when you have done it.

Fred Osborn
Episcopal Church Foundation

—— SO-47 ——

Parish Newsletter–*Good News*

We send our church newsletter, *Good News*, free of charge, to the entire church membership. We have a volunteer lay editor, who does this as a part of her stewardship. I make sure that I read it before it is sent out so that I will know what is happening in the church and in the diocese. We send it out twelve months of the year–the church does not take a vacation, only its clergy and the people do. The newsletter is sent out by a special mailing team.

This morning I want to give thanks for our parish newsletter editor and for our special mailing team, who are responsible for the newsletter's being published and delivered to our homes. This letter is especially appreciated by our homebound members, because it connects them to our church and they know they have not been forgotten. Our thanks to all in our church who give their time, abilities, and money to make the good news of Jesus Christ known here at [St. Thomas's] and throughout the world.

ℽ

Our parish newsletter is our way of communicating our life in Christ here at [St. Thomas's]. The newsletter doesn't just happen—it comes to your homes through the faithful stewardship of our editor and our mailing team. They give of their time and abilities to make it happen. Our thanks to all of you who, through your stewardship of time, abilities, and money, enable our church to be a church with good news to spread. Thank you!

— SO-48 —

Presiding Bishop's Fund–Disaster

The Presiding Bishop's Fund is for disaster relief, making grants on a national and an international scale to provide redevelopment after such disasters as the floods in the Midwest and the war in Rwanda.

ℽ

Today we are given the opportunity to make a special offering, above our weekly pledge, that will go to the Presiding Bishop's Fund. We are called by Jesus Christ to care for those in need. Paul took a collection from the Greek congregations when those in Jerusalem were starving. Please be generous.

ℽ

[*St. Thomas's*] is committed to changing the world. We believe that if our church should disappear tomorrow, it would be missed and the world would be a poorer place. Today, through our stewardship, we have a chance to make a difference in our world. Our offering demonstrates our love and compassion for those far beyond our own congregation. I know you will be generous. Thank you!

―― SO-49 ――

Reformation Sunday

In the Presbyterian Church, Reformation Sunday is celebrated on the last Sunday of October. It is an occasion to remember one of the hallmarks of our Reformation heritage, our belief that the church reformed is continuously being re-formed by God for God's purposes.

Today is a time to look backward and forward. We recognize that we are here today–that we have heard the good news–because of the faithfulness of generations that have gone before us. We are able to read the Bible because of those who preserved manuscripts and made God's word available to others. We sing hymns written hundreds of years ago. We worship in this place today because of the vision of other Presbyterians who saw the possibilities for a congregation on Providence Road, and our sanctuary is enhanced by a pulpit and communion table bequeathed to us by another congregation, no longer in existence. All of this represents faithful stewardship.

As we look to the future and what God is doing with and through us, let us pray that we will be as faithful as those who have preceded us. In the words of the hymn we will sing shortly: "Let courage be our friend, Let wisdom be our guide, as we in mission magnify the Crucified! In bold accord, come celebrate the journey now and praise the Lord!"

Let us celebrate and praise the Lord through our gifts and our offerings of thanksgiving.

The Rev. Mary Doyle Morgan
Maryland Presbyterian Church USA

─── SO-50 ───

Sabbatical

St. Thomas's provided two months for a sabbatical for me–two weeks in the Holy Land at St. George's College in Jerusalem and six weeks at Virginia Theological Seminary to write the first draft of this book.

∽

Today, as I prepare to leave for [*insert location*], I want to thank you personally for my sabbatical. It is through your generosity that I am able to go to study, reflect, write, and refresh my ministry here among you. It is your stewardship and commitment to my growth and renewal that have made this possible. Please keep me in your prayers that I may make wise use of my time, abilities, and money.

∽

Tomorrow I will be leaving for my sabbatical, made possible by our governing board and your generosity in both spirit and money. I thank you for the faithful giving of time, ability, and money that you have invested in our future together here at [*St. Thomas's*].

─── SO-51 ───

Seekers' Service I

At the Community Church of Joy, there are special services for "Seekers"–those searching for a relationship with Jesus Christ through worship in the church. These services offer an alternative to the "Believer Services" of the Church of Joy. These minisermons are offered by Tim Wright, Executive Pastor of the Church of Joy, who is responsible for the worship at the Seekers' Services.

∽

This past week Joy conducted five funeral services—all of them for people who did not attend our church. They provided us with the opportunity to share the love of Christ with people at a time of loss and brokenness. Thanks to your faithful financial support, Joy was able to make a difference. Because of you, great ministry like this happens everyday. Thank you. Keep up the good work!

The Rev. Tim Wright
Community Church of Joy
Phoenix, Arizona

෭

The ministry of the Community Church of Joy exists because of the generous financial support of our members and friends. We do not get our funds from any sources other than our Sunday offering. It is your giving that enables us to provide excellent Sunday School classes for children, support groups, counseling, aid for those in need of food or clothing, and above all, exciting inspiring worship. Your giving is making a difference. We encourage you to continue being a part of the great work God is doing through us!

The Rev. Tim Wright
Community Church of Joy
Phoenix, Arizona

— SO-52 —

Seekers' Service II

The Bible tells us that God loves us so much that He gave His very best—He gave Jesus. And in response to that great gift, we have the opportunity to say "Thank you," to God by giving Him a portion of ourselves through our financial gifts each week. As we give, we honor God, and we participate in His mission of letting others know about Jesus.

The Rev. Tim Wright
Community Church of Joy
Phoenix, Arizona

෭

At this time, we are going to receive the offering. This is the time when the members and friends of Joy, through their giving, help underwrite and support this ministry. If you are visiting with us today, we want you to know that you are under no obligation to participate in the offering. You are our guests. We are glad that you are here and we invite you to join us again just as soon as you can. To those of you who are family and friends of Joy, we want to invite you to continue your generous and faithful support.

The Rt. Rev. Tim Wright
Community Church of Joy
Phoenix, Arizona

——— SO-53 ———

Seminary–Theological Education

In 1982, the General Convention of the Episcopal Church passed a 1 percent resolution–that 1 percent of the net disposable income of each parish be given to a seminary of the Episcopal Church. We include $1,500 in our budget to be divided between my alma mater and our associates' seminaries. In most parishes, including my own, however, we do not communicate this contribution well.

ɷ

Today is the closest Sunday to January 25, Saint Paul's Day. Traditionally, this is Theological Education Sunday. We here at [*St. Thomas's*] include [*insert amount*] in our budget for [*insert names of schools*]. A percentage of your offerings on Sunday goes to support men and women preparing to serve God in both the lay and ordained ministries. On their behalf, I thank you for your generosity.

ɷ

This morning, we have with us [*insert the name of guest*] from [*insert name of school*]. We support [*name*] and [*his/her*] class-mates at [*insert school name*], as well as students at [*insert the names of any other schools the church supports*], through every Sunday's offering. It is our commitment to the future of our church and the quality of the ordained and lay ministries. Thank you who give so generously, week by week.

SO-54

Soup Kitchen–Paul's Place

Through our Love Boxes, Outreach Fund, and volunteer efforts, our church supports an Episcopal-Ecumenical Soup Kitchen in Southwestern Baltimore. We now make box lunches for one hundred people each month.

Today I want to share with you one of the fine Good Samaritan ministries we here at [*St. Thomas's*] support through our stew-ardship of time, abilities, and money. Through your generous offerings, the homeless and hungry of [*insert name of town or city*] will eat this week. Jesus told us to feed the hungry and we are doing that because of your generosity.

This past week, a group of eleven volunteers went down to Paul's Place to prepare and serve lunch and then to wash up, clean the tables, and sweep the floor. In your name, we looked into the eyes of the hungry and, on your behalf, we received many heart-felt "Thank You's!" You should feel good about this ministry–it is an outgrowth of your generous giving. Thank you!

—▸ SO-55 ◂—

Stewardship Sunday

On Stewardship Sunday, the parishioners are asked to bring their pledge cards to church and, as families, bring the cards to the altar when they come for communion. Stewardship Sunday is a joyful day of worship.

◯

Today, when you come to the altar for communion, please bring your pledge cards with you and place them in the Alms Basin, which will be here in the middle of the chancel. Our commitment of our pledge of money is an acknowledgment that all we have is a gift from God, and we are choosing to honor God by returning to God a portion of what we have received for the work of Jesus Christ through our church. Thank you for your commitment to God through [*St. Thomas's Church*].

◯

Today we celebrate and acknowledge with thanksgiving all of God's gifts to us. We are honored to make our commitment to God's work for next year through [*St. Thomas's Church*]. We joyfully acknowledge the source of all goodness and life, and respond by our offering of our pledges this morning as we come forward to receive the Bread of Life. After we have all given our pledges, we will stand and praise God by singing the *Doxology*. Thank you for your faithful stewardship.

—— SO-56 ——

Stewardship is Your Own Business

I was a very young vicar working with a fairly new steward-ship committee. We were altogether determined somehow to reach those families that never pledged or that never kept up with a pledge. The stewardship consultant we approached was of no help to us in this at all. He even said to us that we were working on the "wrong" people. He had the gall to say that we should first of all start with ourselves! Good Christian stew-ardship does indeed begin with ourselves. It begins with "Me!" It is "My business!" It is the Heavenly Father's business. "All things come of thee, O Lord, and of thine own have we given thee."

The Rt. Rev. C. L. Longest
Episcopal Suffragan Bishop of Maryland

—— SO-57 ——

Stewardship Witnesses

On the Sunday preceding Stewardship Sunday, at both of our Sunday morning services, we have two lay persons witness to their practice of stewardship.

⌒

This morning, I want to thank [*insert names*] for witnessing to their personal stewardship. It was gratifying to hear how they and their families are giving out of grateful hearts in thanksgiv-ing for all of God's blessings. During the coming week, you are being asked to pray about your financial stewardship to God, through your church family. Your decisions will decide the future of our parish for next year. I pray that we are becoming a tithing church and that we may continue to have the resources to pro-claim Jesus Christ as our Lord and Savior.

⌒

You have heard the witness of [*insert name*] and [*insert name*]. Later this week you will receive a letter with a pledge card and envelope from our stewardship chairman. I ask you to pray alone or as a family about your pledge to God for [*insert year*] through [*St. Thomas's Church*].

What you commit to God's work here will decide the future of your church. Will we continue to reach out in the name of Jesus and grow, or will we be held back and shrink? The choice is yours. May God, through the Holy Spirit, guide you in your decision this week. Next Sunday we will gather and give thanks for your pledges in a service of celebration and thanksgiving.

—— SO-58 ——

Tithing I

Tithe, a five-letter word, is as close as you can get in the Christian church to a four-letter word—mention it and Christians rise up in protest! However, it *is* Episcopalian. At the 1982 General Convention and at conventions ever since, the following resolution was passed: "The tithe is the minimum standard of giving by Episcopalians for God's work." Teach it, and it will make a difference in the lives of your church members. It is best, however, to talk about this at a time that is not related to Stewardship Sunday. Learn your own denomination's position on the tithe.

∞

Each Sunday we pass the collection plates and give our offerings. The question we all need to answer for ourselves and our families is: "How much should we give out of all that has been given us for God's work?" Our church uses as the standard "the biblical tithe" as the minimum for our giving. I pray that the standard is our standard now, or that we are moving toward that tithe. Thank you for your disciplined giving, week by week, for God's work through [*St. Thomas's Church*].

∞

In a few moments, the ushers will pass the collection plates among us and in them we will place our offerings to God. I want you to consider the tithe as the minimum standard for giving to carry out God's work. We believe we are doing God's work here. We ask you for generosity, in a disciplined way, to support us that we may continue this task. Thank you for choosing our church as your primary way of returning to God a portion of what has been given you.

———— SO-59 ————

Tithing II
Good Stewards of All God Has Given Us

God is the source of all things. God calls us to be accountable, as any steward is accountable, for all the things that God has given to us. We are accountable for 100 percent of all that we have in our possession. That means all of our time, our talents or gifts, and our money. Tithing helps us to manage better that 100 percent. To be able to tithe absolutely requires that we learn to manage well all that we have and all that we are. Every one of us can learn about money, about ourselves, about God as we grow in our ability to be good stewards of all that God has given us.

The Rt. Rev. C. L. Longest
Episcopal Suffragan Bishop of Maryland

———— SO-60 ————

United Thank Offering

Twice a year, in the fall and spring, we mail out special envelopes with our newsletter, and they are also made available from the ushers. This United Thank Offering, called UTO, goes out of the parish, traditionally given by women for missionary work by the church. *Note*: Always publish the amount given and remember to say "Thank you."

Today we will collect the United Thank Offering. It was originally "for women only," but women soon recognized that men could
be thankful, too. It represents pure thanksgiving for all God's gifts
to us. Your offering to UTO, along with your regular offering, provides us with a way to say "Thank you" to God. This special offering goes for ministry in our nation and world, in our name.

I have here a United Thank Offering envelope. To explain to new
members of our church, these envelopes are mailed out every
spring and fall. They are an individual and family offering in
thanksgiving for all of God's gifts to us and are used for missionary work in the United States and around the world. I do
hope that all of you will be part of this offering. Traditionally, it
provides a way to fund our missionary work of Christ, over and
above our regular offerings.

—— SO-61 ——

Vestry Conference

Following the vestry elections in the spring, the vestry of St.
Thomas's Church, the clergy, and a paid consultant go off together for a vestry-rector evaluation. It is a time for an unhurried
review of last year's goals and objectives so as to set new ones for
the coming year. It is a time to develop a healthy relationship
between vestry, clergy, and parish. In this way, molehills do not
become mountains!

This coming Friday and Saturday, the vestry and clergy will be
going to a conference center for our annual clergy-vestry evaluation. Many Sundays, we pray that our vestry will make wise use
of our offerings–the money we give to God through [St. Thomas's
Church]. This conference is a time for us to examine the way our
parish is living our mission–"The worship and service in Jesus'
name,"–and our vision. Please keep us in your prayers, as our
vestry practice their stewardship of time, ability, and money.

Yesterday our clergy and vestry returned from our overnight retreat. I want to thank the vestry for their excellent use of their own stewardship of time and abilities. It was a wonderful experience for me to see *your* vestry and *your* clergy working together to review, plan, and engage in creating our mission and vision for [*St. Thomas's Church*] for the coming year. Thank you for your stewardship of time, abilities, and money–your gifts enable us to be a church that is living the mission.

—— SO-62 ——

Vestry Elections

At St. Thomas's, we have competitive elections for the vestry, our governing board. Normally, between six and nine people stand for election each year. Three are elected. We display their pictures on a tripod at the entrance to the church and a short biography of each candidate is printed in the newsletter.

Tonight, we will be electing the men and women who will serve as members of our church's vestry to lead our parish. We are thankful for those members of our parish who, as a witness to their stewardship, have consented to stand for election. We here at [*St. Thomas's*] appreciate the hard, faithful work of our vestry. They practice their stewardship with their time–they are in church every Sunday, their abilities–they serve the parish in many ways, and their money–everyone pledges and supports God's work through [*St. Thomas's Church*].

In this week's bulletin you can find the biographies of the men and women who are standing for election to serve on the vestry. I want to commend them for their stewardship and their saying "Yes" to giving their time, abilities, and money, to accept the mantle of leadership in our parish. Our thanks to you, the members of [*St. Thomas's Church*], who, by your faithful stewardship, enable our vestry to carry out our mission and vision.

SO-63

Vision–Church

The Vision Statement of our church reads: We are a church of Jesus Christ, in which all people are welcome, every member is a minister, the world is our responsibility, disciple-making is our goal, and worship is our duty and delight.

We cannot accomplish any part of our Vision Statement without your generosity. When joining the church, we pledged to "faithfully participate in the church's ministries by our prayers, our presence, our gifts, and our service."

Thank you for your past gifts, and let us look forward to the wonders that can be accomplished by the guidance of our Vision Statement and our giving our offerings through love.

Catherine A. Ritter
Towson United Methodist Church
Towson, Maryland

SO-64

Wedding–The Following Sunday

In the Episcopal Church, a couple normally is required to attend at least three premarital counseling sessions, then the wedding rehearsal, and, of course, the wedding itself.

Yesterday, I witnessed and blessed the marriage of [*insert names*]. It was a joyful day! I thank you for your faithful stewardship that enabled me to meet with them for premarital counseling sessions, have a fun wedding rehearsal, and then to gather here yesterday with their family and friends. They came here as strangers, and through your love and acceptance, they have become members of our church family. Thank you again for your generous gifts, for you are building a Christian community.

Yesterday, here at our altar, [*insert names*] had their marriage witnessed and blessed. They know that this is their spiritual home. Thank you for your generous gifts each Sunday. Your giving enabled me to be available to meet with them to prepare them for their marriage. Your gifts provided a beautiful, holy place for them to gather yesterday and celebrate this event. Your faithful gifts of time, abilities, and money are building a Christian community. Thank you!

——— SO-65 ———

Welcoming Committee

Our Welcoming Committee is responsible for welcoming all who come as strangers to [*St. Thomas's Church*]. They act as greeters, stand with the clergy after services, take pictures of newcomers and post them on our Newcomers' Bulletin Board together with brief biographies, and act as "buddies" to new families, introducing them to the rest of the congregation. All but one of them have been in the parish for less than three years, so each one can easily remember what it was like to be "the new kid on the block."

Today, as part of our stewardship, I want to thank our Welcoming Committee members at [*St. Thomas's*]. They meet you after the service, standing next to me at the door. They take the pictures for our Newcomers' Bulletin Board, and their special ministry is welcoming the stranger. But we realize that welcoming the stranger is part of every baptized member's ministry. This is one significant way we here at [*St. Thomas's*] practice our stewardship of time, ability, and money. The five-year-old child reaches out to a new child in kindergarten class. You greet someone new after church or visit over a cup of coffee during Hospitality Hour. These are the ways you serve, and you are the reason that our church is growing. Thank you.

This morning, [*insert name*] will be taking pictures of our newcomers for the Newcomers' Bulletin Board. We are thankful for all those whom God is bringing to our church "to worship and serve in Jesus' name with us. I thank you for your faithful stewardship of your time, ability, and money. By your generous giving of each, you are helping [*St. Thomas's*] live out its mission. Thank you!

———— SO-66 ————

Wills–Bequests–Planned Giving I

"The Minister of the Congregation is directed to instruct the people, from time to time, about the duty of Christian parents to make prudent provision for the well-being of their families, and of all persons to make wills, while they are in health, arranging for the disposal of their temporal goods, not neglecting, if they are able, to leave bequests for religious and charitable uses."
Book of Common Prayers, page 445

∞

Today I want to read to you the following passage which explains what I am expected to do [*see above*] You need to have a will. Your heirs need for you to have a will. It is your responsibility to care for your family. As you are part of our family here at [*St. Thomas's Church*], I pray that you will also remember us generously, as much as you are able to do so.
(Read from the Prayer Book
the passage found on page 445.)

∞

A will is your final statement of your Christian stewardship. I thank God for those of you who have remembered [*St. Thomas's Church*] in your wills. Your faithful stewardship in planning for your death has strengthened our parish immeasurably.
(Again, read from the Prayer Book
the passage found on page 445)

SO-67

Wills–Bequests–Planned Giving II

When the church receives a bequest, this good news should be shared with the congregation. At St. Thomas's, we have received bequests each year.

This past week, we received a bequest from [*insert name*] for [*insert amount*]. [*His or her*] generosity is welcomed. The vestry has placed a 10 percent tithe with the Outreach Fund and the remainder with the Heritage Fund. Through the Outreach Fund, [*his or her*] gift will enable [*St. Thomas's*] to help those in need and, through the Heritage Fund, to care for our church. Our thanks to all who remember our church in their wills.

This past month, we received a generous bequest of [*insert amount*] from [*insert names*]. Their family has explained that their wishes were that it be used for our physical plant. We have tithed 10 percent to our Outreach Fund, and the remainder will be used to install a new public address system and to cover all the facia with aluminum to beautify our outside, as well as to make it maintenance free. Our thanks to them and to all of our parishioners who, as part of their stewardship, have remembered [*St. Thomas's Church*] in their wills.

CROSS REFERENCES AND INDEX

Scripture–Cross Referenced

Luke

∞

John

∞

Old Testament

∞

New Testament

∞

Sermons–Cross Referenced

Church Year

Special Occasions

∽

Contributors–Cross Referenced

The Rev. Phebe Coe
Church of the Epiphany
Odenton, Maryland
SO-33 page 82
SO-34 page 83

The Rev. Roy W. Cole
Interim Specialist for
    Revitalization
Diocese of Maryland
G-19 page 34
G-20 page 35
G-21 page 36
G-22 page 36
G-23 page 37

Canon David W. Crockett
Episcopal Diocese of Western
    Massachusetts
G-16 page 32
G-17 page 33
G-18 page 33
CY-14 page 51

Dr. Amelia J. Geary
Center for Teaching
Virginia Theological Seminary
Alexandria, Virginia
SO-2 page 56
SO-9 page 61

The Rt. Rev. Robert Ihloff
Bishop of the Episcopal Diocese
    of Maryland
CY-7 page 43
CY-9 page 46

The Rt. Rev. Charles Longest
Suffragan Bishop of the Episcopal
    Diocese of Maryland
SO-56 page 102
SO-59 page 104

Bishop George Mocko
Delaware/Maryland Synod
Evangelical Lutheran Church in
    America
SO-35 page 84

The Rev. Mary Doyle Morgan
Maryland Presbyterian Church, USA
Towson, Maryland
SO-37 page 85
SO-49 page 96

Frederick Osborn
Episcopal Church Foundation
New York, New York
SO-41 page 89
SO-42 page 90
SO-43 page 91
SO-44 page 92
SO-45 page 93
SO-46 page 94

The Rev. Ronald Reed
St. James Episcopal Church
Wichita, Kansas
CY-15 page 52
SO-20 page 70
SO-36 page 84

Catherine A. Ritter
Towson United Methodist Church
Towson, Maryland
SO-23 page 73
SO-63 page 107

The Rev. Tim Wright
Community Church of Joy
Evangelical Lutheran Church
    of America
Phoenix, Arizona
SO-51 page 97
SO-52 page 98

BIBLIOGRAPHY

Scripture quotations, unless otherwise noted, are from the New Revised Standard Version Bible, copyright 1989 by the Division of Christian Education of the National Council of the Churches of Christ in the USA and used by permission.

Excerpts from the *Book of Common Prayer* (BCP) 1979, copyright by Charles Mortimer Guilbert as Custodian of the *Book of Common Prayer*, 1977, used by permission.

Quotation from *Giving and Stewardship in an Effective Church: A Guide for Every Member*, copyright 1992 by Kennon L. Callahan, reprinted by permission of HarperCollins Publishers.

Quotation from *Soul and Money: A Theology of Wealth* by W. Taylor Stevenson, used by permission of the Office of Stewardship of the Episcopal Church Center.

Quotation from *The Challenge of the Disciplined Life: Christian Reflections on Money, Sex and Power*, copyright 1985 by Richard J. Foster, reprinted by permission of HarperCollins Publishers.

The poem "The Bustle in the House," from *The Complete Poems of Emily Dickinson*, edited by Thomas H. Johnson, published by Little, Brown and Company. Used by permission.

Excerpt from the poems "The Leaden Echo" and "The Golden Echo" by Gerard Manley Hopkins from *Poems in Prose*, selected and edited by W.H. Gardner, published by Oxford University Press. Used by permission.